Virtue by Design
Illustrated Chinese Children's Books From
The Cotsen Children's Library

Don J. Cohn

Cotsen Occasional Press

Virtue by Design: Illustrated Chinese Children's Books From The Cotsen Children's Library

Published by Cotsen Occasional Press, Los Angeles, California. The material illustrated in this book is the property of the Cotsen Family Foundation, Los Angeles, California.

Printed in Hong Kong

© Cotsen Family Foundation, 2000

Text: Don J. Cohn
Editor: May Holdsworth
Production: Edgar Chiu
Layout & Design: Roy Hui
Photography: Lou diGiacomo
Printer: Mantec Printing Company

The author would like to thank Meng Lei for enlightening and lightening the burden, and May Holdsworth, Ivy Trent, Harriet Shapiro and Gopal Sukhu for reading the manuscript and offering valuable suggestions.

ISBN 0-9666084-3-7

Front cover picture:
How the Brain Works, see page 36.

Back cover picture:
A Visitor from Outer Space. Wall poster, 1980.
The boy with the rocket propulsion device on his back might be seen as a reincarnation of Mr. Science from the May Fourth movement. The dialectic between science and knowledge on the one hand, and democracy on the other, has been a recurring motif in Chinese politics in the 20th century.

DEDICATION

In memory of my late wife JoAnne S. Cotsen for starting me on an international quest for children's books.

With appreciation to Don Cohn whose knowledge of China's language, culture and people not only made it possible to amass most of the Chinese juvenile material in the Cotsen Children's Library but who also illuminates the sampling of it represented in these pages.

And to the countless Chinese writers and artists whose creations reveal the changes wrought in their culture even as they introduce it to their young.

Lloyd E. Cotsen
Los Angeles
December 1, 1999

CONTENTS

Illustrated Guide to Eye Exercises

A Note on the Captions

Classifications, titles and bibliographical details, where known, are in bold type, with titles in italics.

Background information on the illustrations, descriptions of the pictorial content or glosses are in roman type.

Translations of the Chinese captions or text printed on the illustrations are in italics.

Traditional Chinese books, and some later publications, are read from right to left.

CONTENTS

Dedication by Lloyd E. Cotsen — iii

A Note on the Captions — iv

Preface — 1

Introduction — 3

A Selection from the Cotsen Children's Library — 19

Early Primers and Glossaries — 20

Early Pictorial Material — 24

1910s–1920s — 28

1930s — 34

Japanese Occupation — 40

1940s — 42

The Seventeen Good Years 1949–66 — 48

Cultural Revolution 1966–76 — 74

Post-Cultural Revolution 1977–99 — 86

Bibliography of English-language Sources — 91

PREFACE

The Chinese holdings of the Cotsen Children's Library consist of more than 35,000 items from mainland China, Taiwan and Hong Kong. The collection comprises the entire range of printed matter a child might encounter in his or her daily life. Primers, textbooks, song books, arts and crafts handbooks, dictionaries, supplementary readers, wall posters and slides from the school classroom, comic books, magazines, newspapers, riddle and puzzle books, board games, cigarette cards, and cram-school manuals for extracurricular reading are all part of the library's Chinese collection, as are nursery rhymes, fairy tales, science fiction and adventure stories for bedtime reading.

The collection spans four centuries, from the late Ming dynasty (1368-1644) to the present day. The earliest books, primers, glossaries and various versions of the Confucian classics are printed from hand-carved woodblocks on soft paper and bound between flimsy covers with silk thread. In the late 19th century, modern presses for lithography and copper engraving came into use in Shanghai and Canton, cities with significant foreign populations. These presses, originally imported by Christian missionaries, produced the classroom posters and color plates the appear frequently in textbooks of this period.

Virtue by Design concentrates on illustrated books, periodicals and other printed matter, presenting more than 200 pictures arranged chronologically. The principal criteria for the selection of the pictures are visual interest and the power of the illustration to represent a particular period, ideology, concept or political movement. These pictures chronicle the history of Chinese society, revealing the values, fashions and tastes of the time. They also provide information about social class, discipline, etiquette, family structure, dress, architecture and cuisine.

In China, a single image can represent an entire period or movement. For example, one of the most widely-distributed books of all time, the "Little Red Book," a collection of brief excerpts from from Mao Zedong's writings, is the prime literary icon of the Cultural Revolution (1966-76). During this period, the very same pictures of posturing proletarian heroes, children engaged in class struggle, and peasants and soliders acting as classroom teachers appeared in nearly every book, magazine, film, drama and wall poster. In fact, a single 16-page issue of *Little Red Guard* magazine serves as a miniature catalog of the entire range of propagandistic art and dominant ideologies of that tumultuous decade.

The one important area of the Chinese holdings of the Cotsen Children's Library not represented in this book are early 20th-century periodicals devoted to educational practice and theory. Many of these magazines, none of them illustrated, are published by provincial or municipal boards of education, and record the numerous debates about education that took place as China evolved from empire to republic to communist state. The Cotsen Children's Library is one of the few institutions in the United States to have these unique periodicals.

One particular aim of the Chinese collection of the Cotsen Children's Library is to show the impact of politics on children's books published from the late "Mao Zedong period" (1949-76) to the "Deng Xiaoping period" (from 1978 to the present). Both reigns are amply represented in the present book.

PREFACE

The majority of this collection was purchased from dealers and at flea markets and antiquarian book shops in Beijing and Shanghai, where the trade in old and used books caters to both foreigners and Chinese. Government-run Xinhua and educational bookstores throughout China, including Xinjiang and Tibet, supplied the most recent publications. The rare-book trade in China is unsophisticated and unorganized, the very opposite of that in Japan and the West. Furthermore, there are few dedicated collectors or specialized collections of early children's books. Judging from their public catalogs, even major libraries in Beijing and Shanghai have limited holdings of Chinese children's books and periodicals. There remains in China today a vague taboo surrounding acknowledgements of positive contributions made to Chinese society by the Japanese presence in China (1931-45), the puppet state of Manchukuo, and the Republic of China under Chiang Kai-shek during periods of conflict with the Chinese Communist Party. A similar taboo surrounds books and magazines published during these years. Many were destroyed. These factors point up the difficulty of studying the history of Chinese children's books in China today, and the importance of building collections of such material outside the country.

On the other hand, since the end of the Cultural Revolution and the opening of China in the late 1970s, Chinese scholars and writers have begun a re-examination and re-evaluation of traditional Chinese culture. Publishers have cranked out a vast range of popular and academic books dealing with every conceivable aspect of traditional Chinese culture, from eunuchs to cricket-fighting. These books include new editions of the early classical primers, histories of education and studies of children's literature. Luxury versions of the classical novels and such tomes as *The Twenty-Four Dynastic Histories* in cartoon form for young people are aimed at China's first generation of only children, many of whose parents were deprived of a formal education during the Cultural Revolution.

Virtue by Design is a small showcase of representative Chinese items in the Cotsen Children's Library, a remarkable, visionary collection that ranges from cuneiform tablets to Nazi propaganda and includes countless treasures in between. It is hoped that the present volume will highlight the need for a study of the entire range of printed matter produced for Chinese children.

Don J. Cohn
Beijing and Hong Kong, January 2000

INTRODUCTION

The study of children's books and children's education in China takes us back to dynastic times. The Chinese invented writing approximately 6000 years ago, paper around 1800 years ago, and the printed book in the Tang dynasty (618–907). Unique among world writing systems for its age and continuity, the corpus of Chinese characters in use today was adopted by the imperial court from a range of variants in the short-lived Qin dynasty (221–206 BC).

From ancient times, the state has played a key role in education in China. In the words of historian Marianne Bastid, "In China education has...always been explicitly integrated within a set of political and social conceptions. Whether it aimed at fostering virtue or at forming men of affairs for leadership, it had a function within the State. It was to ensure a certain social order."[1] The persistence and omnipresence of ideology, be it the canon of Confucian values, the tenets of modern nationalism or Marxist dogma clearly reinforces this claim.

Primary schools in traditional China were set up variously by local officials, clans, and private families for their children. A teacher was hired, and a room converted to a school, with little more furniture than some hard benches and desks, and possibly an image of Confucius. The teacher, or *xiansheng*, literally "first-born" or "respected elder," was in most cases poorly paid but enjoyed the respect of the community. He—such teachers were almost always men, although mothers taught their children at home—was likely to have been a *shengyuan*, a holder of the lowest degree in the imperial examination system, who could not hold office.[2]

The education of young children in China was, until the 17th century, mostly funded by private sources. Only in the late Ming (1368–1644) and Qing (1644–1912) dynasties did the government establish community and charitable schools, especially in border regions where the influence of Han Chinese culture and language was weak, but also in densely populated regions. Yet the fact that schools were privately run did not prevent some of the poorest elements of the population from attending. The benefits of an education could extend to youngsters who were not direct members of the clan or social unit sponsoring the school. Despite a prevailing "open admissions" policy for those who were intelligent and desired an education, some schools refused enrollment to the children of prostitutes, actors and menial workers such as woodcutters and servants.

Classroom poster. Editorial Department, Ministry of Education, 1907–08. *Honor thy teacher.*

Classroom poster. Editorial Department, Ministry of Education, 1907–08. *Brothers.*

INTRODUCTION

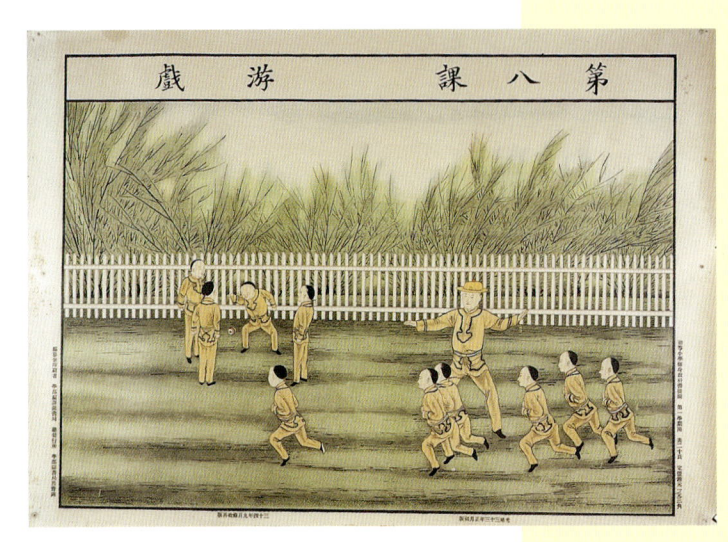

Classroom poster. Editorial Department, Ministry of Education, 1907–08. *At play.*

Classroom poster. Editorial Department, Ministry of Education, 1907–08. *A happy family.*

Young students started to attend school at the age of six or seven. After mastering a number of short texts, typically the *Thousand Character Classic*, the *Trimetrical Classic* and *Hundreds of Surnames*, they would advance to the nine pillars of the Confucian canon, the so-called "four books and five classics," including the *Analects* of Confucius, *Mencius*, *Book of Changes*, *Book of Songs* and *Book of Rites*.

The ultimate purpose of the bookish and impractical education derived from the Confucian classics was, for the elite, to prepare for the civil service examinations that placed boys and young men in the official bureaucracy, the most respectable occupation in traditional Chinese society (girls were banned by imperial decree from sitting for these examinations). The examination system, first instituted in rudimentary form in around 200 BC, during the Han dynasty, flourished in the Tang (618–907) and Song (960–1279) dynasties. A modern system of civil service examinations only replaced this venerable institution in 1905.

The principal method of learning in China, from ancient times to the present day, is rote memorization, or "stuffing the duck" as it is called. The popularity of this method is due in part to the nature of the Chinese written language, which has no equivalent to the easily-mastered Western alphabet, and to the nature of the examination system, which required lengthy citations from the classics. If the written language of a total of some 4000–5000 characters is broken down into its basic graphic components, there are about 500 distinct forms, but these are never learned in a systematic way. While rote learning is widely criticized by modern Chinese writers as "uncreative," under the traditional system, pupils could learn 2000 different Chinese characters of the literary language in their first year of school simply by memorizing the three most popular texts mentioned above, thus laying a solid foundation for further study. It has been estimated that in the course of a traditional education, a boy would memorize texts with a total of 400,000 characters.

The 3000-year-old classical language used in these texts remained the principal medium of education and the examination system up until the early 20th century, although primers in the vernacular were published in the Ming and Qing dynasties. But it was not until after the May Fourth movement of 1919 that the vernacular began to replace the classical language in Chinese textbooks, although this transformation took several decades to achieve throughout China. The 1920s also saw the emergence, for the first time in Chinese history, of literature

INTRODUCTION

especially written for children. Yet the moral and didactic tone of the early texts continues to prevail in textbooks written in the modern period.

THE THREE PRIME PRIMERS

The first textbook that children were likely to read is the *Thousand Character Classic (Qian zi wen)*, written in the Liang dynasty (502–552) and arguably the world's earliest primer. Composed of 1000 different Chinese characters in 250 four-word rhymed phrases—a significant act of literary virtuosity in itself—the text teaches the basics of astronomy, climate, history, ethics, food, agriculture and common knowledge in elegant classical Chinese. According to legend, the author wrote the book in a single evening at the request of the emperor; by the next morning, the author's hair had turned completely white. He was, however, compensated generously for his efforts.

The *Millenary Classic*, as it is also called, begins:

> The heavens are of a somber hue; the earth is yellow;
> The whole universe was one vast waste.
> The sun reaches the meridian and declines; the moon waxes and wanes.
> In divisions and constellations the stars are arranged.
> Heat and cold alternatively prevail.
> The autumn is for ingathering, and the winter for hoarding up...
>
> Of vegetables, the most valuable are mustard and ginger.
> Sea water is saline, and river water fresh.

First page of the *Thousand-Character Classic*. No place of publication or date given, *ca.* 1920.

This is followed by a synopsis of Chinese history, after which the text takes a moral turn:

> Observe and imitate the conduct of the virtuous,
> And command your thoughts that you may be wise.
> Your virtue once fixed, your reputation will be established;
> Your habits once rectified, your example will be correct.[3]

The *Trimetrical Classic (San zi jing)*, or *Three-Character Classic*, probably written in the Southern Song dynasty (1127–1279), consists of 376 three-character phrases (the total number of words varies with different editions) formed into pithy statements about psychology, education and human relationships. A long opening section gives a chronology of Chinese history, with lists of emperors both mythological and historical. Model youths from ancient times are praised, such as a boy who tied his long hair

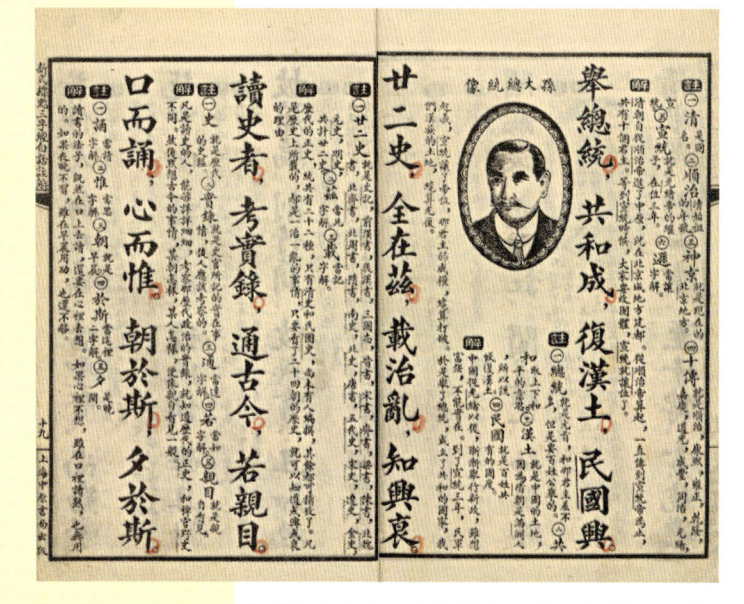

***The Trimetrical Classic, Illustrated and Explained in the Vernacular.* Zhongyuan Book Company, Shanghai, 1926.** This revised version brings the historical section up to the early years of the Republic (1912–49). The illustration is of Sun Yat-sen, the "father of the Republic."

INTRODUCTION

to a ceiling beam to prevent himself from falling asleep while studying, and a masochistic counterpart who pierced his own buttocks with an awl whenever he was about to doze off over his books.

Here are the famous first lines translated by the great sinologist Herbert A. Giles in 1910, when the book was still universally read in China:

> Men at their birth, are naturally good;
> Their natures are much the same; their habits become widely different.
> If foolishly there is no teaching, the nature will deteriorate;
> The right way in teaching is to attach the utmost importance to thoroughness....
>
> To feed without teaching is the father's fault;
> To teach without severity is the teacher's laziness.
> If the child does not learn, this is not as it should be;
> If he does not learn while young, what will he be when old?
>
> If jade is not polished, it cannot become a thing of use;
> If a man does not learn, he cannot know his duty towards his neighbor.
> But he who is the son of a man, when he is young should attach himself to his teachers and friends and practice ceremonial usages.[4]

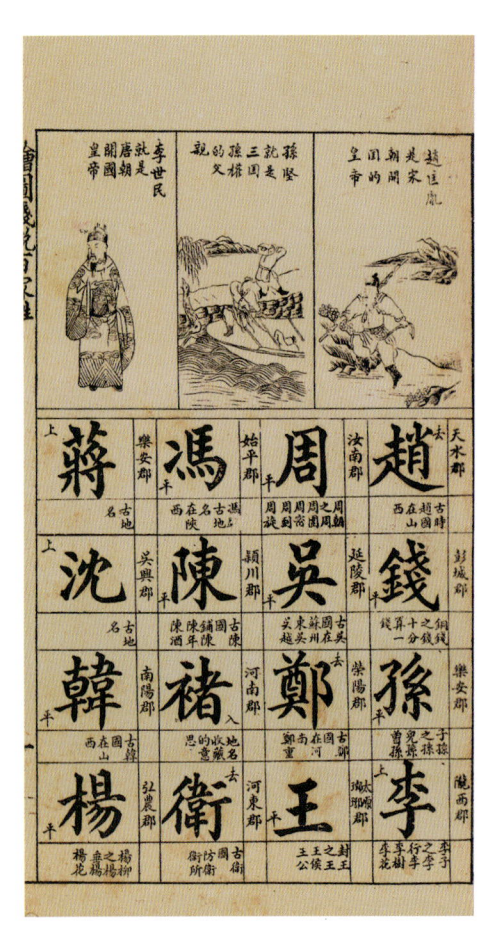

First page of the *Hundred Surnames, Illustrated and Annotated with a Brief Commentary*. Yangjia Academy, Shanghai, 1906.

The Hundred Surnames (*Bai jia xing*), more accurately translated as *Hundreds of Surnames*, attributed to an author of the Northern Song dynasty (960–1127), is a list of 504 single- and double-character surnames, arranged in groups of four, with the last character in the even-numbered lines rhyming. In the earliest editions, the first surname in the text is Zhao, the family name of the Song emperors. In the Ming dynasty, Zhao was replaced by Zhu, the family name of the new occupants of the dragon throne. The Qing-dynasty emperors in turn replaced Zhu with Kong, the surname of Confucius (in Chinese, Kong-fu-zi); their own clan's Manchu surname, Aisin-Gioro, would have spoiled the rhyme scheme. The first 32 surnames (the rhyming characters are shown in bold) in the standard version are:

Zhao	Qian	Sun	Li
Zhou	Wu	Zheng	**Wang**
Feng	Chen	Chu	Wei
Jiang	Shen	Han	**Yang**
Zhu	Qin	You	Xu
He	Lu	Shi	**Zhang**
Kong	Cao	Yan	Hua
Jin	Wei	Tao	**Jiang**

During the Ming and Qing dynasties, a host of primers and short anthologies for young learners was published. These include collections of poetry such as the *Poems of One Thousand Authors (Qian jia shi)* and *Poetry for Prodigies (Shen tong shi)*, anthologies of literature, history and geography such as *The Children's Primer (Xiao Xue)*, *Dragon Texts and Shadows of the Whip (Longwen bianying)*, *Stories from the Emerald Grove for Study by Youngsters (Youxue gushi chonglin)*, *The Twenty-four Examples of Filial Piety (Ershisi xiao)*, and a wide range of illustrated dictionaries and illustrated glossaries.

There were also books especially for girls, the best known of which is *The Classic for Girls (Nü er jing)*, written in the Qing dynasty. Beginning in the Ming dynasty, children supplemented their education by reading the great historical novels, including the *Outlaws of the Marshes (Shuihu zhuan)*, *Journey to the West (Xiyou ji)* and *Romance of the Three Kingdoms (Sanguo yanyi)*, all favorites of Mao Zedong, who quoted from them frequently in his writings.[5]

Despite their nearly universal distribution and profound influence, it should be noted that in terms of content all of the books described above are not children's books as we know them today. Rather their purpose was to expose children to the elementary building blocks of the vast establishment of Chinese traditional culture, of which language was an essential component.

FILIAL PIETY EXEMPLIFIED AND EXCORIATED

To demonstrate the graphic and rather perverse nature of some of these books, two of *The Twenty-four Examples of Filial Piety*, a much reprinted and highly influential book written by Guo Jujing in the Yuan dynasty (1279–1368) are given below. The archaism of the 19th-century translation conveys the stilted flavor of the original:

> In the Chau [Zhou] dynasty (1066–221 BC), there flourished the venerable Lai, who was very obedient and reverential toward his parents, manifesting his dutifulness by exerting himself to provide them with every delicacy. Although upward of 70 years of age, he declared that he was not yet old; and usually dressed himself in parti-colored embroidered garments, and like a child would playfully stand by the side of his parents. He would also take up buckets of water, and try to carry them into the house; but feigning to slip, would fall to the ground, wailing and crying like a child: and all these things he did in order to divert his parents.

From *The Twenty-four Examples of Filial Piety, Illustrated in Color.* **Sine Laboratory Co., Ltd. Shanghai, 1939.** *The venerable Lai entertains his aged parents.*

From *The Twenty-four Examples of Filial Piety, Illustrated in Color.* **Sine Laboratory Co., Ltd. Shanghai, 1939.** *Wu Mang encourages mosquitos to bite him to protect his parents.*

INTRODUCTION

> Wu Mang, a lad eight years of age, who lived under the Tang dynasty (618–907), was very dutiful to his parents. They were so poor that they could not afford to furnish their bed with mosquito-curtains; and every summer's night, myriads of mosquitos attacked them unrestrainedly, feasting upon their flesh and blood. Although there were so many, yet Wu would not drive them away [and thus let them bite him], lest they should go to his parents, and annoy them. Such was his affection. [6]

Some other examples worth mentioning include a son who tastes his father's stool in order to aid in a medical diagnosis; a high official who takes great pains to clean his mother's chamber pot every night; a man who attempts to bury his three-year-old son alive because there is not enough food to feed his mother; and a son who lies down naked on a frozen pond to melt the ice, enabling him to catch a pair of carp to provide food for his step-mother, who despises him.

The Twenty-four Examples of Filial Piety was extremely popular. The Cotsen Children's Library has illustrated examples of the text in the form of wall posters, sets of hanging scrolls, cigarette cards, colorful tracts distributed free of charge by shops as well as a number of early Qing-dynasty illustrated editions.

In an essay entitled *The Twenty-four Examples of Filial Piety, Illustrated*, Lu Xun, one of the most important Chinese writers of the 20th century, pointed out some of the absurdities and dangers of this book:

> The first picture book I ever owned was a copy of *The Twenty-four Examples of Filial Piety, Illustrated*, a gift from a relative… It seemed that everyone knew the stories in the book. Even people who couldn't read…only had to look at a picture in the book, and they could reel off the whole story in great detail. Though possessing this book made me very happy at first, my feelings soon changed. After I got someone to read the 24 stories to me, I realized that being "filial" was an impossible ideal. Thus at an early age I gave up all hope of becoming a filial son.
>
> …When I was younger and more innocent, acting in a "filial" manner meant being obedient and taking orders from my parents. I also knew that when I grew up, I would have to ensure that my aged parents had enough to eat. But once I started reading the book, I realized that this had nothing to do with being filial, and that acting in a filial way was actually many dozens or even many hundreds of times more difficult….
>
> The stories I found most incomprehensible, to the point of being offensive, were *Venerable Lai Entertains His Parents,* and *Guo Ju Buries his Son*…. What upset me [about the first story] was the line about Venerable Lai "feigning to slip" and falling to the ground. Few children, regardless of whether they are rebellious or obedient, intentionally "feign" things, nor do they enjoy listening to stories that are mere rumors or scandalous. Anyone who has even the most elementary understanding of child psychology knows this. [7]

Cover illustration of *Little Red Guard Pictorial*, March 1, 1973.
Lei Feng on duty.

INTRODUCTION

In modern times, the spirit of filial piety to one's parents has been extended to love of China, the Communist Party, and at different times, the Chinese leadership. The honor of The Twenty-fifth Example of Filial Piety clearly belongs to Lei Feng (1942–64), a People's Liberation Army soldier who died in an accident while on duty during a lightning storm. Lei's self-abnegating vow to "be content to remain a screw in the revolution" became the subject of several mass propaganda campaigns, the first of which was launched by Chairman Mao with the simple dictum: "Study Lei Feng's good example." Books and posters extolling Lei Feng's almost mythical virtues remain in print today.

Lu Xun was not the only critic of the traditional curriculum in classical Chinese. His views were shared by many other intellectuals of the Republican period, including his brother Zhou Zuoren and the art historian Zheng Zhenduo. Their attitude toward traditional culture had been formed when they studied in Japan during the early decades of the 20th century. To these men, both the language and content of the classical books were obstacles to modernization that had no relevance to contemporary society.

Writing in 1935, for example, the editor Wu Yanyin attacked the entire traditional curriculum for its impracticality with a sarcasm typical of his generation:

> Some of these books [in the traditional Confucian cannon] were not even conceived as educational texts. The ideas in some of them are simply impossible for children to understand. And the concepts in them have very little relevance to children's lives. The language in which they are written is so convoluted, dense and profound, that not even repeated reading and recitation from memory will give the student an understanding of the material. It takes a boy seven or eight years just to get through the basic Confucian corpus... Students could spend their entire lives studying such books, pouring over them until they drew their last breath, and still fail to understand what they were reading.
>
> Although a person who devoted a lifetime to the study of these books could eventually hone himself into the intellectual curiosity known as a "complete Confucian scholar," only a tiny number of true geniuses could accomplish this feat. But in fact those rare geniuses usually turned out to be eccentrics or human freaks, pedantic and muddleheaded bookworms who could barely distinguish an apple from a pear. Or they would end up as arrogant and pretentious oddballs known as "scholarly gentlemen"...

A panoramic presentation of *The Twenty-four Examples of Filial Piety* in the form of a label for cloth manufactured by the Dagong Dyeing and Weaving Factory. Printed in Shanghai *ca.* 1935.

INTRODUCTION

> Compared to geniuses and prodigies in the West, who grow up to become inventors and scientists…and contribute to the progress of their countries, the Chinese phenomenon of the "complete Confucian scholar" is all the more pathetic and lamentable. With the establishment of a modern school system, the Confucian corpus should gradually disappear from children's reading lists and be replaced by proper primary school textbooks that can provide children with intellectual nourishment capable of increasing their wisdom.[8]

Japanese coeducational classroom as illustrated in a late-Meiji period ethics textbook published in 1903.

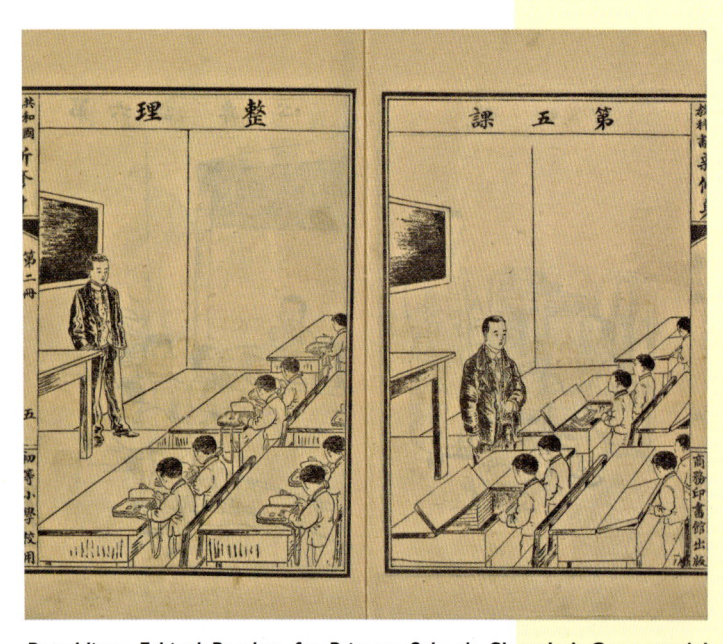

Republican Ethical Readers for Primary Schools. Shanghai, Commercial Press, 1912. *Putting one's things in order.*

FOREIGN INFLUENCE

The provision of such nourishment had begun in earnest following China's defeat in the Opium Wars (1839–42) and with the growing presence in China of Western missionaries who opened schools alongside their churches. Another stimulus to revising traditional methods of education came from the Meiji Restoration of 1868 and the implementation of Western-inspired modern education in Japan in 1872. This led to the rapid modernization of the country, which culminated in Japan's victories in the Sino-Japanese War of 1894–95, and the Russo-Japanese War of 1904–05. Chinese students flocked to Japan in the late 19th century, and were deeply impressed with the country's efforts at modernization and borrowing from the West. In the field of education, the main influence came from England and Germany.

The first Chinese Ministry of Education was established in 1903, and one year later modern schools opened with a curriculum and system of administration similar to that of Japan. But the Japanese influence, primarily authoritarian and based on an imperial state, waned following the fall of the Qing dynasty in 1911.

The publication of government-approved textbooks at this time became one of the major activities of newly established publishing companies that were to nearly monopolize the field for the first half of the 20th century. The Commercial Press (founded in 1897), the Chung Hwa Book Company (1903) and the World Book Company (1921) became China's leading publishers. In fierce competition for the children's book market, these presses tried to outdo each other by issuing large numbers of textbooks, magazines and literary anthologies, which explains the remarkably high quality of children's literature and art during this period. In the 1920s, The Commercial Press and Chung Hwa Book Company, both based in Shanghai and hence heavily influenced by Western publishing practices, accounted for 70 per cent of all textbooks published in China.

The country-wide political and cultural movement that began as a demonstration in Beijing on May 4, 1919 was a search for ways to modernize China and to regain national pride. One outcome of the May Fourth Movement, as it was called, was the replacement of the classical language by the vernacular form. Chinese education thereafter turned to a more liberal Western, specifically American, model, which enjoyed a brief heyday in the early 1920s. Pointing to the incompatibility between Confucianism and modern society, with its emphasis on intellectual freedom and human rights, a writer introduced two concepts which he called "Mr. Science" and "Mr. Democracy," mascots that would usher China out of its imperial past into the modern world.

From the time of the May Fourth movement up to the Japanese invasion of 1937, political instability in China was reflected in rapid shifts in educational policy, which in turn led to the publication of new textbooks that ranged across a broad political spectrum. Yet the textbooks of the time remained faithful to their mission of indoctrinating students in the spirit of modern nationalism.

PEOPLE'S CHINA
In 1949, the new People's Government and the Chinese Communist Party were faced with the enormous task of consolidating a poor and undeveloped country that had been rent by revolution, world war, and civil war for most of the 20th century. In the field of education they drew upon two decades of experimentation with socialist education that had begun in the Jiangxi Soviet (1929–34) and continued in "liberated areas" in the border regions—havens against Japanese control—where the soldier-peasant cultural bias could be perpetuated, notably at the communist stronghold in Yanan.

The communist takeover of China had a powerful effect on the publishing industry. Following the flight of Chiang Kai-shek and his government to Taiwan, Kuomintang civics textbooks were burned as part of a gradual ideological cleansing. Furthermore, "over 90 per cent of books published by the large Commercial Press of Shanghai were burned, dumped or pulped"[9] during the early years of the People's Republic. Publishing houses for children were established in Shanghai, Beijing and elsewhere to restock bookstores and replace the contents of libraries, schools and home bookshelves. Under the red banner of Communist China, children's publishing became a regular conduit of party doctrine and ideology.

The greatest single influence on education in New China came from the Soviet Union, the Chinese Communist Party's "Big Brother" from the 1920s

Cover illustration of *Learning Chinese Characters by Looking at Pictures*. Qiming Bookstore, Shanghai, 1952. Education in the countryside in the young People's Republic.

INTRODUCTION

until the Sino-Soviet split in the late 1950s. In the early 1950s, the Soviet middle-school curriculum was translated into Chinese and transplanted to China. By 1954 "some four million Soviet texts had been received."[10] The system of children's palaces and the institutions of the Young Pioneers (for children nine to 15) and Communist Youth League (for young people 15 to 25) replaced earlier children's and youth organizations.

To give a specific example of the priorities of the new regime, here is a memorandum listing four key areas in the curriculum of an elementary school in Nanjing around 1950:

1. Lectures on the superior culture and the abundant local products of the motherland, and on the greatness of the strength of the motherland and on the elevation in her international position in order to cultivate in the child a high degree of national self-respect and self-confidence and to cause him to love his motherland.

2. Instruction on the historical facts of aggression against, and oppression and exploitation of, peoples by imperialism, feudalism, and bureaucratism, to cause the child *to hate the enemy* [italics added], particularly American imperialism and the Kuomintang reactionary clique.

3. Introduction of the main points of the Common Program, to cause the child to know the correct leadership of the Chinese Communist Party and of Chairman Mao, as well as to love the Communist Party and Chairman Mao.

4. Explanation of the great strength of the world peace camp to cause the pupil to know that the Soviet Union is the fortress guarding the peace of the world, that Stalin is the leader of the peaceful peoples of the world, and (to cause him) to love the Soviet Union, Stalin, and the laboring peoples of the world.[11]

Calendar supplement to the January 1963 issue of *Children's Epoch* magazine, commemorating the 300th issue. *Children of Every Ethnic Minority Group Deeply Love Chairman Mao.*

Following these guidelines, some of the themes that recur from 1949 to 1966 (often referred to as the "seventeen good years" before the beginning of the Cultural Revolution), are the Korean and Vietnam Wars, with a strong anti-American, anti-imperialist bias; praise of the 1957 Great Leap Forward and the establishment of the people's communes; reiteration of the vow to "liberate" Taiwan; adulation of model revolutionary heros such as the soldier Lei Feng and the peasant girl Liu Hulan; sympathy for revolutionary struggles in the Third World; and a strong stress on the importance of physical and manual labor in childhood education.

The emphasis on science also reappeared in the 1960s, though without an accompanying insistence on democracy, in the quest

to launch a satellite to keep up with the Soviet Union.
The exaltation of Chairman Mao and the memorization of his essays and sayings, even before the advent of the "Little Red Book" during the Cultural Revolution, appeared in virtually all printed media for children. Pupils studied Mao's essays from the Yanan period, including the best known three: *The Foolish Man Who Moved Mountains, In Memory of Norman Bethune* (a Canadian physician who served in China during the Yanan period) and *Serve the People.* These texts attained biblical status; children and adults memorized them, sang and danced to them.

CULTURAL REVOLUTION AND RESOLUTION
In addition to the social and political chaos of the Cultural Revolution, the anarchic decade saw the complete rewriting of all books, the closing down of numerous periodicals and the persecution of leading authors and editors. Schools remained closed for months or years as student Red Guards divided into factions and cliques persecuted ("struggled") their teachers, parents and friends. Factional conflict in schools and universities resulted in the deaths of thousands of young people, and the People's Liberation Army was brought in during the most violent moments of the period to quell the chaos. Mao Zedong, who launched the Cultural Revolution in order to purge reactionary elements from the party, later realized and admitted that certain aspects of the revolution had gotten out of hand, but much of the damage that took place—including cannibalism, tank battles on campuses, the hounding of "class enemies" to suicide, widespread and indiscriminate destruction of personal and public cultural property—occurred well beyond the control of the central government in Beijing.

Teachers were publicly humiliated by their students, academic achievement was derided as bourgeois, and workers, peasants and soldiers were upheld as revolutionary models, the true social avant-garde. Students were encouraged to copy their classmates' work to avoid enhancing any particular individual's reputation. Book learning and all traditional means of education were reviled and mocked. A popular saying went: "In primary school dead serious about reading books. In middle school read dead books seriously. In the university seriously read books to death." In hospitals, doctors cleaned toilets while janitors performed surgery, their proletarian class backgrounds qualifying them for this work. To counter "bourgeois laziness," physical and manual labor became compulsory in all schools for both staff and students. Even kindergarten pupils "sat around tables for an hour a week testing torch bulbs with batteries before slotting them into cardboard frames; they stuck brown paper together to make shoe bags…"[12]

Cover of the comic book, *Ten Heroes of the Sichuan-Tibetan Highway Who are Forever Faithful to Chairman Mao.* People's Art Publishing Company, Beijing, 1970.

Page from *Ten Heroes of the Sichuan-Tibetan Highway*
In August 1967, the Great Proletarian Cultural Revolution developed with rapid ferocity. Armed with the weighty cudgel of Mao Zedong Thought, one hundred million soldiers and civilians smashed the bourgeois headquarters under the direction of Liu Shaoqi, the notorious traitor, enemy within the ranks and scab. At this moment, Assistant Political Instructor Li Xianwen was leading the Eleventh and Twelfth Battalions on a mission to deliver war materiel to the border area.

INTRODUCTION

Children's text, Don't Allow Lin Biao to Carry Out Revisionism. Beijing, 1974.
In a 1973 campaign to "criticize Lin Biao and Confucius," Mao's one-time designated successor was posthumously victimized for sharing the ideology of "revisionist" Confucius. The ancient Chinese sage had advocated a return to the values, or "rites," of the past. Lin Biao apparently died in a plane crash in 1971 following a failed attempt on Mao's life. In the text, children are encouraged to use their pens as weapons to write criticisms of Lin Biao and Confucius.

Little Red Guard magazine. Shanghai, November 10, 1976. Published several months after the death of Mao Zedong, the contents include a song praising the wisdom of Hua Guofeng, Mao's appointed successor, and an article condemning the radical Gang of Four.

The Cultural Revolution decade, which has yet to be addressed publicly in China in a serious manner, is extraordinarily well documented by a huge corpus of factional newspapers, political tracts, wall posters, books and magazines, many of them characterized by the extensive use of red ink. In these publications, much space is devoted to the unassailable moral virtue of Mao Zedong and his image, writings and calligraphy. After the "Little Red Book" of Chairman Mao's selected sayings and other little red books containing his essays, poems and speeches, the most popular reading matter for youngsters were the small rectangular comic books (*xiao'er shu*), which contained entertaining but politically correct stories about historical figures or modern heroes. For Chinese who were of school age during the Cultural Revolution when the schools closed, these comic books served as language textbooks, and were often the only books they had to read.

The death of Mao and the fall of the leftist faction known as the Gang of Four in 1976 brought the Cultural Revolution to a swift end. Over the next two years, China was ruled by Hua Guofeng, a Mao look-alike and his chosen successor. In 1978 the political rehabilitation of Deng Xiaoping heralded the onset of China's opening up to the outside world, a process still continuing with the re-emergence of civil society, bourgeois values, and "capitalism with Chinese characteristics." Through the 1980s, ideological concerns gave way to a stress on the "Four Modernizations" (agriculture, industry, defense and science/technology), and a mass movement to spread scientific knowledge. Democracy was again notably absent from the Modernizations, which were little more than a revival of the theme promoted in the May Fourth Movement and again during the 1960s. Education regained its former place in the Chinese value system, and teachers were praised for their contribution to society and with some fanfare received conspicuous salary raises. There is no greater symbolism of the restoration of "normality" in China as the appearance of an anonymous bespectacled Shanghai intellectual alongside a peasant woman and a miner on the Chinese 50 renminbi banknote first issued in the 1980s.

INTRODUCTION

Fifty-renminbi note, People's Bank of China, 1990. The gentleman to the left of the peasant woman and miner is an elegant stereotype of a Shanghai intellectual, complete with spectacles, white hair and Western coat and tie.

In the 1980s and 1990s, China saw unprecedented economic growth accompanied by rising incomes and expectations. The publishing business has grown increasingly commercial and less ideological, yet the Chinese Communist Party retains a tight hold on education and the content of textbooks. Illustrations in children's textbooks, magazines and other printed matter during this period are characterized by their cuteness, garish colors and a *faux* sense of intimacy between artist and reader. These pictures obviously draw their inspiration from television, video games and Japanese *manga* comic books, as well as from trends in Taiwan, Hong Kong and the United States. The use of color printing is widespread, but the overall quality of books is low. Overt borrowing of foreign models suggests a brewing Chinese identity crisis, as well as an open-minded approach to the world outside of China.

***Good Children* magazine. Shanghai, November 1, 1979.** Published after the rehabilitation of Deng Xiaoping, who replaced Hua Guofeng as Communist Party chairman.

GAMES AND AMUSEMENTS

Although the books described above share a serious and didactic moral tone, childhood in China was leavened by numerous toys, games, puzzles and other forms of amusement. In school, children learned Chinese characters by means of sets of wooden blocks, each with a different character carved or printed on it, or used picture cards with the Chinese word for the depicted object printed on the front or the back. Children collected cigarette cards during their heyday in China in the first two decades of the 20th

INTRODUCTION

Tangrams for Young Children. **Basic Bookstore, Shanghai, 1954. Translated from a Russian children's book.** *Pistol, heavy machine gun, cannon.*

Detail from uncut set of story cards entitled *We Must Definitely Liberate Taiwan* **published in Shanghai by the Meiwen Paper Products Company,** *ca.* **1960.** Brief captions are printed on the back of each picture.

century. While accumulating a complete set was the goal of the collector, the cards, illustrated with pictures of *The Twenty-four Examples of Filial Piety*, traditional professions, or characters from famous novels, also served an educational purpose.

Perhaps the best known Chinese game, or puzzle, is the tangram (*qi qiao ban*), a set of seven small geometric shapes made of wood or paper that are combined to form simple pictures of plants, animals, household objects, or people performing various tasks. Tangram books contain several hundred finished figures either in outline or silhouette form, the challenge being to assemble the pieces into the illustrated result. By the early 19th century, the tangram puzzle was well known throughout Europe, and was possibly played by Napoleon during his exile on the island of Helena.

An early type of gambling game with educational purposes is *Sheng guan tu*, awkwardly rendered as "Chart of Promotion Through the Official Hierarchy," or "Peking Pecking Order." This board game, played with dice, consists of a series of squares that proceed in rows from the edge of the paper towards the center in a "square spiral." Each square represents a different official rank and, in the versions illustrated on page 24, contains a portrait and the name or title of the person depicted. The goal of the game is to progress through the ranks on the way to the highest official position of prime minister, the square in the middle of the board. Perhaps the notion of placing the imperial palace or Chinese emperor's dragon throne in the winning square would be considered lese-majesty. One example of this game in the Cotsen Children's Library, undated but from its contents obviously from the early 1950s, is based on the government structure of the newly established, post-Republican People's Government.

PERIODICALS

The more than 10,000 Chinese periodicals in the Cotsen Children's Library fall into two categories. The first consists of national, provincial, prefectural (county-level) and municipal journals published for teachers and school administrators. These professional

16

INTRODUCTION

journals deal with questions of educational reform, curriculum, teaching methods, foreign trends in education, child psychology and other practical and theoretical issues. Most date from the Republican period (1912–49).

The second group includes magazines for children, ranging from some of the earliest examples of this genre, published around 1900, to the 1980s. Magazines of the Republican period, many of which ceased publication during the Sino-Japanese war of 1937–45, reveal the strong nationalistic strain evident in education and culture in general, as well as broad and unbiased borrowing and influence from Europe, America and Japan in terms of content and illustrations. Among the finer publications are *Children's Knowledge (Ertong zhishi)*, published by the Children's Book Company (Ertong shuju) in the late 1940s, *Children's Graphic Magazine (Ertong huabao)* and *Children's World (Ertong shijie)*, both published beginning in 1922 by the Commercial Press. Some of these periodicals ceased publication during the Japanese occupation, resumed publication in the 1940s, and changed format after the founding of the People's Republic in 1949.

One of the rarer periodicals in the collection is *New Youth* (*Xin shaonian*, not be confused with the important Communist Party journal, *Xin qingnian*), a Chinese-language magazine for boys published by the Japanese in Beijing from 1940 to 1945, which was modeled after the influential Japanese boy's magazine, *Shonen Club*.

Probably the most important and longest running children's magazine is *Xiao pengyou* or "little friends," the term used by adults to refer to children other than their own. First published by the Commercial Press in 1922, it is still popular today. *Xiao pengyou* and another magazine, *Children's Epoch (Ertong shidai)*, produced by the China Welfare Association under the patronage of Soong Chingling (1892–1981), the wife of Sun Yat-sen, are particularly noteworthy for their fine illustrations.

During the Cultural Revolution, regional editions of *Little Red Guard* (*Hong xiao bing*) were issued in more then 15 cities and provinces, with different contents. Other children's magazines were published in the larger cities, notably Tianjin's *Little Red Guard*

***Xiao pengyou* magazine, November 26, 1958.** Photograph of children collecting scrap metal for "backyard" blast furnaces during the Great Leap Forward.

***Children's Epoch* (*Ertong shidai*) magazine, June 1, 1965.** The illustration, entitled "Heroic Vietnamese Tiger Hunter," depicts a Vietnamese peasant girl and her prey, a "paper tiger" (false threat) with the name Johnson (referring to U.S. president Lyndon Johnson) inscribed on its right paw.

17

INTRODUCTION

Pictorial (*Hong xiao bing huabao*). These magazines either changed names or ceased publication at the end of the Cultural Revolution.

CONCLUSION

In the 20th century, China has undergone several major revolutions: the revolution of 1911, which overthrew a dynastic system more than 2000 years old; the communist revolution, which resulted in the implantation of a foreign ideology that still sits uncomfortably in the East Asian setting; the Cultural Revolution, an act of political upheaval; and the opening of China to the West—a Great Leap Outward, as it were—which resulted in a high level of interdependence between China and the outside world that is unprecedented in modern times. The Chinese holdings of the Cotsen Children's Library illustrate these turbulent, always traumatic changes in a dramatic, graphic manner.

In Chinese society, where the traditional values of filial piety have been transmuted into subtle and outright forms of nationalism, the child is very much father to the man. A critical examination of the books, magazines and posters in the collection reveals directly, not through a crystal ball, the thinking processes of China's present and future leaders.

Poster. "People's Liberation Army soldiers: what fine marksmen you are!" Ca. 1980.

Notes

1. Ruth Hayhoe and Marianne Bastid, Editors. *China's Education and the Industrialized World: Studies in Cultural Transfer.* Armonk, New York and London: M.E. Sharpe, Inc., 1987
2. Evelyn Sakakida Rawski. *Education and Popular Literacy in Ch'ing China,* Ann Arbor: The University of Michigan Press, 1979
3. Unattributed translation from *The Chinese Recorder,* Volume 4, 1835. Pp. 229-243
4. Herbert A. Giles, editor and translator. *Elementary Chinese: The San Tzu Ching.* Shanghai: Kelly & Walsh, 1910. The present text is taken from an undated Taiwan reprint, *ca.* 1975
5. John Cleverley. *The Schooling of China: Tradition and Modernity in Chinese Education.* Second Edition. Sydney: Allen & Unwin, 1985, 1991
6. Translated in *The Chinese Recorder,* Volume 6, 1837
7. Translation by Don J. Cohn
8. Translation by Don J. Cohn
9. John Cleverley. *The Schooling of China*
10. John Cleverley. *The Schooling of China*
11. Charles Price Ridley, Paul H.B. Godwin, Dennis J. Doolin. *The Making of a Model Citizen in Communist China.* Stanford, California: The Hoover Institution Press, Stanford University, 1971
12. John Cleverley. *The Schooling of China*

A SELECTION FROM THE COTSEN CHILDREN'S LIBRARY

Early Primers and Glossaries

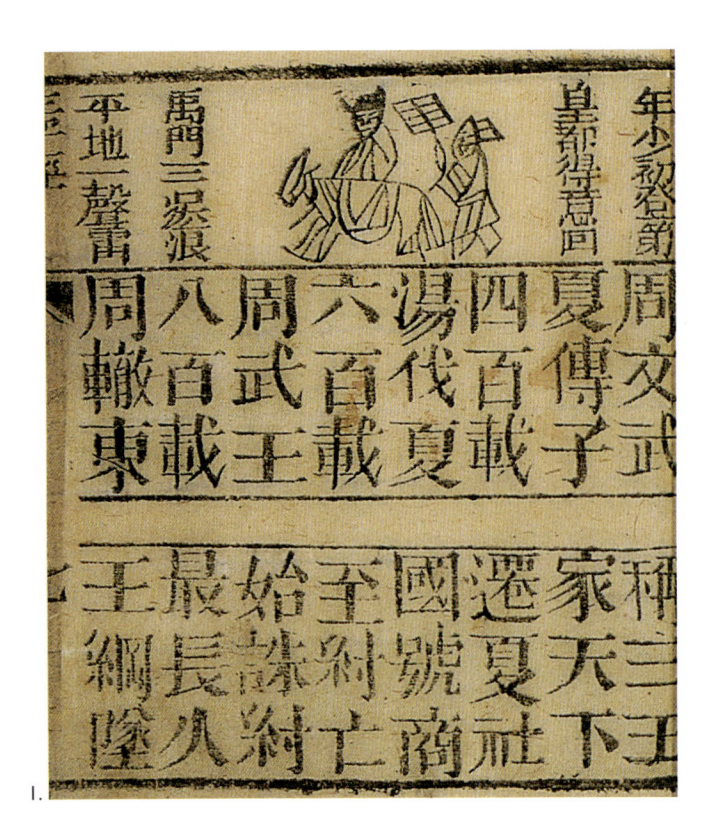

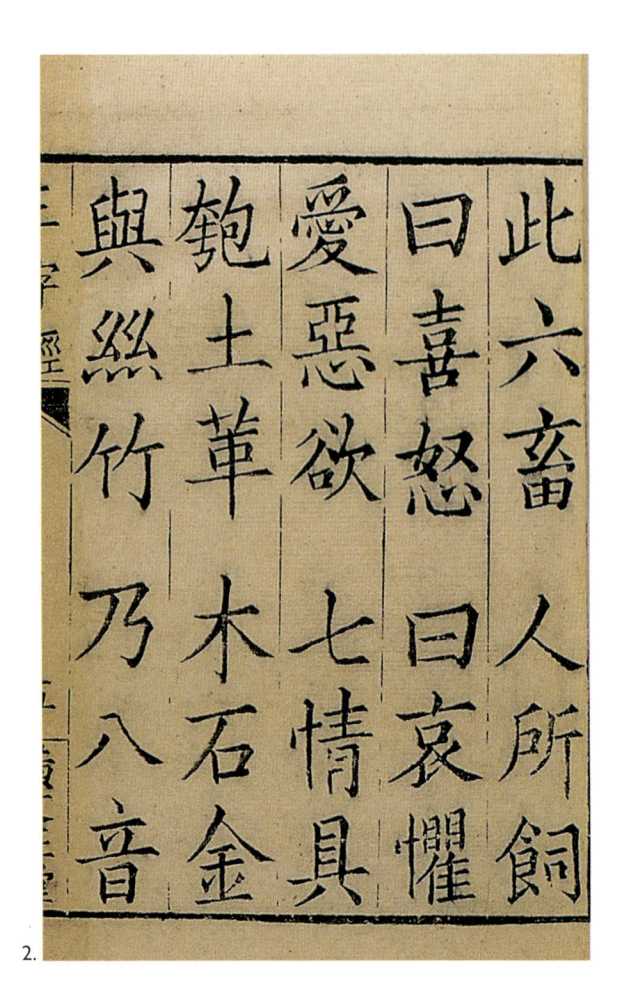

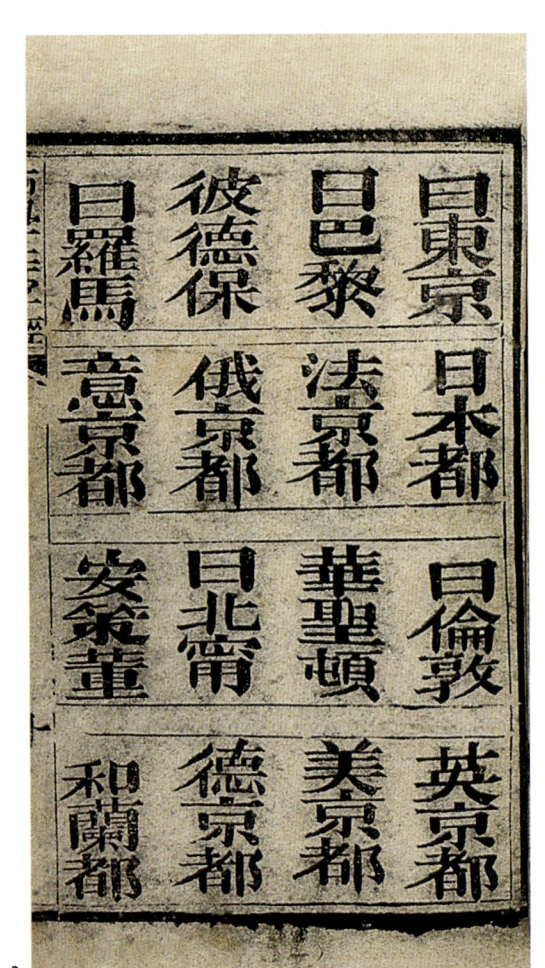

1. **The Trimetrical Classic, with additional content. Published by Wenkueitang, no place, no date, *ca.* 1900.**
The text of the classic is printed in large characters in the two lower registers. The illustrations and a running commentary in the upper register are not directly related to the text below, which is a chronology of the early emperors of the Zhou dynasty. The two lines of text to the right of the picture serve as its caption: *He was young when he first passed the examinations, and returned with great satisfaction to the capital.*

2. **The Trimetrical Classic, Published by Huangwenzhengtang, no place, no date, *ca.* 1900.**
A standard large-character version of the most important Chinese primer.

3. **Trimetrical Classic of Western Learning. Published by Wendetang, no place, 1905.**
One of many variations on the three-character phrase format, this small volume basically offers a list of countries throughout the world and their capital cities.

The book is read down, starting from the upper right hand corner, with two groups of three characters forming each sentence. Foreign proper and geographical names were transcribed into Chinese characters in the 19th century. For example, on this page, Rome is rendered as Luo-ma, Washington as Hua-sheng-dun, Holland as He-lan, London as Lun-dun. The text reads:

Tokyo is the capital of Japan. Paris is the capital of France. Petersburg is the capital of Russia. Rome is the capital of Italy. London is the capital of England. Washington is the capital of the United States. Berlin is the capital of Germany. Amsterdam is the capital of Holland.

Early Primers and Glossaries

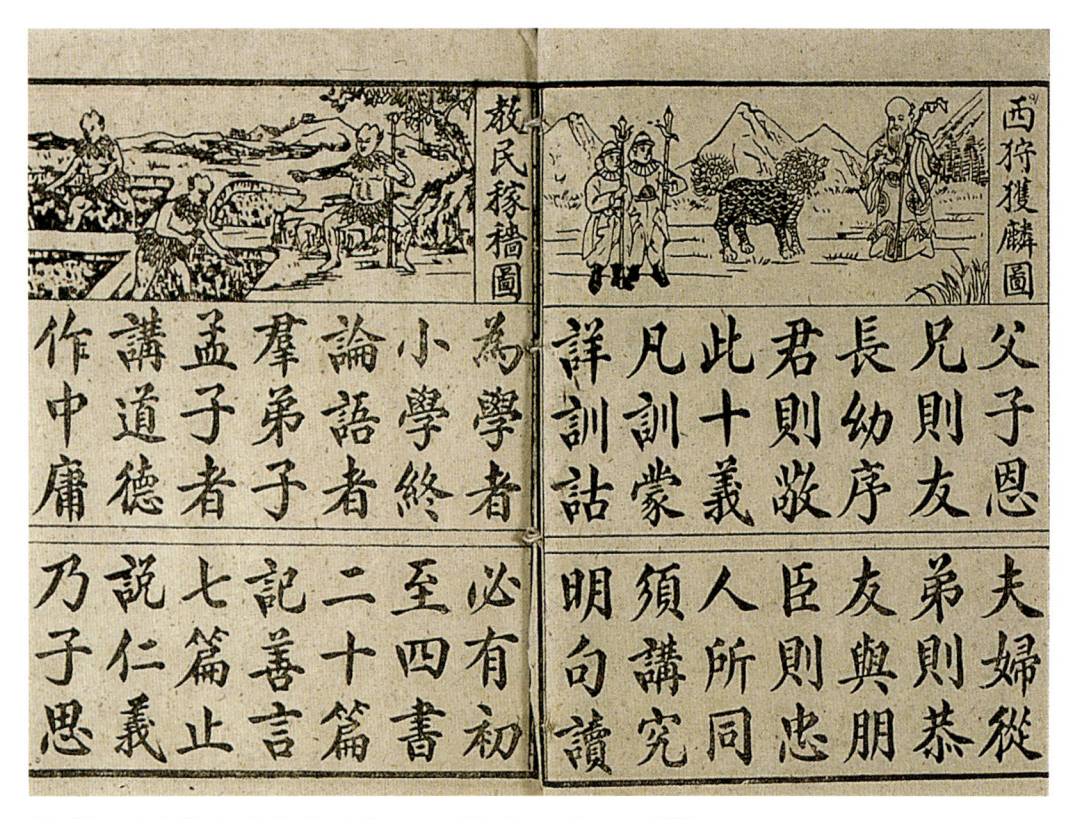

The Trimetrical Classic. Beida Book Company, Tianjin, no date, ca. 1920.
The standard text of the classic is printed in the two lower sections. The upper sections contain illustrations that relate to subjects in the text. On the right, a picture of the founder of Daoism, Laozi, "Going west to capture a kylin." On the left, a picture of the ancient, mythological, immaculately conceived emperor Shen Nong "Teaching the people how to practice agriculture."

Miscellaneous Words for the Education of the Young, in four-character phrases, illustrated. Juguitang, Guangzhou, no date, ca. 1850.
A fully illustrated glossary with pictures and names of objects of daily use, architectural structures, historical figures and other topics. The vertical strings of characters at the top of the page are a topical glossary, divided by subject, and not directly related to the pictures below.

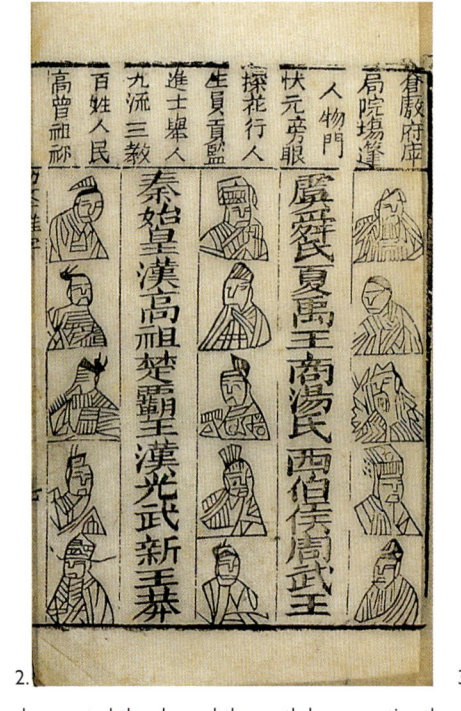

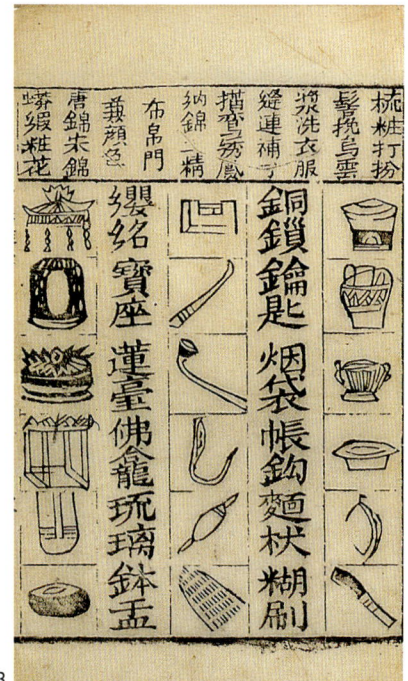

1. Title page and full page illustration of "Pangu, who created the sky and the earth by separating them." In this picture, the sky is below and the earth above.
2. A pantheon of mythological and historical "kings" and emperors, all with imaginary portraits.
3. A selection of objects of everyday use, including a niche for a Buddhist image, monk's begging bowl, bronze lock, curtain hook, rolling pin, coconut shell scoop, clothing iron, brush and razor.

Early Primers and Glossaries

***Illustrated Glossary for Daily Use in Foreign Affairs.* No publisher, no date, *ca.* 1900.**
According to one author, "The [glossaries, *zazi*] circulated among the lower strata of society and were not usually part of the orthodox elementary curriculum. As the regulations of one charitable school state, 'Generally what pertains to orthodox studies should be made primary; all [glossaries] and vulgar books must not be studied.'" Despite this injunction, glossaries were very popular and of great practical use to domestic workers, shopkeepers, traders and others engaged in business.

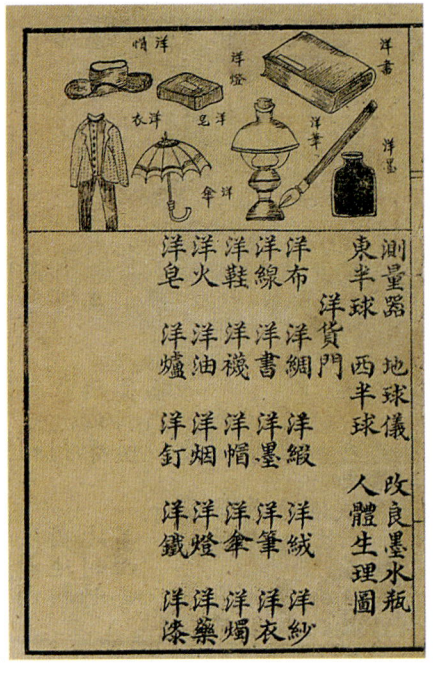

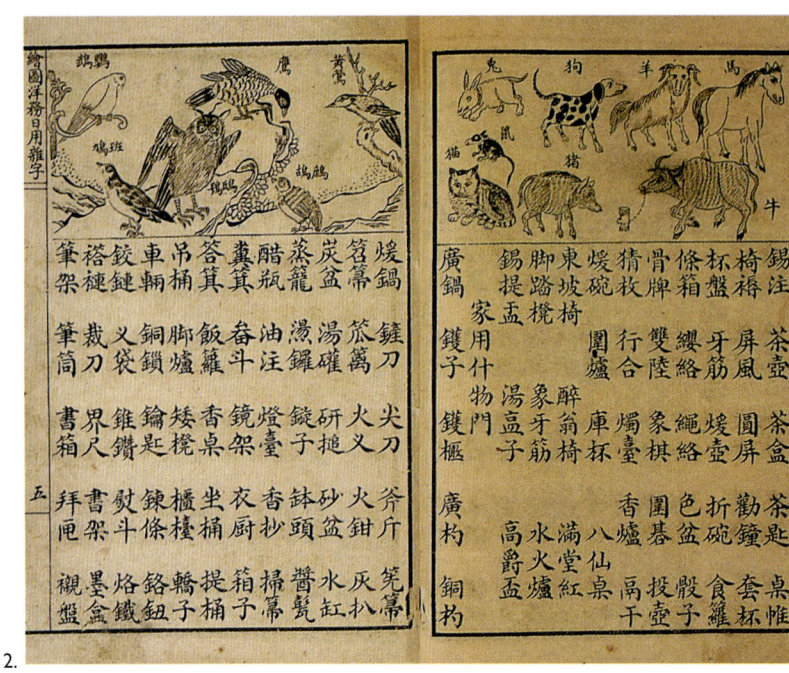

1. The final page illustrates some appurtenances that might be part of the kit of a Western gentleman in China, and might appear in the window of a treaty-port shop. The category "Western" (*yang*, literally, from over the ocean) products includes the following objects, which until recently and still today in a few cases are referred to as Western: calico, matches, kerosene (petroleum), opium, kerosene lantern, galvanized iron.

2. The pictures of "all creatures great and small" do not match the Chinese characters given in the lower section, but the names of the animals are introduced elsewhere in the glossary. The text lists objects of daily use.

***Elementary Reader. Third Edition.* No publisher, no date, *ca.* 1885.**
A textbook from the period of Japanese influence in Chinese education. A principle of Japanese pedagogy is cited in the introduction: "When Japanese pupils learn composition, they are told to describe an object that stands before them. Because of their direct experience with the subject of their composition, the students can build on their own experience in their written work..." Each chapter is followed by comprehension questions.

Catching Fireflies
On a summer night, all the children are enjoying the fresh air in the garden. Each child is holding a fan, and has a gourd-shaped object hanging from his waist. The gourd-shaped objects are made of glass. When the fireflies are placed inside the glass container, they provide a source of light.
  The children agree that they will catch fireflies together, and that whoever catches the most fireflies will be the winner.
  One child ties his fan to the end of a bamboo pole. As a result, he alone captures the fireflies that fly at such high altitudes, and ends up catching the most.
  The other children envy him, and go home to fetch bamboo poles to attach to their fans. But when they return to the garden, it is very cloudy and soon it begins to rain. Thus they catch no fireflies at all.

Questions: Why did the boys have glass gourds tied to their waists? Why was one boy able to catch more fireflies than the others? Why did the other boys fail to catch any fireflies?

Early Primers and Glossaries

1.

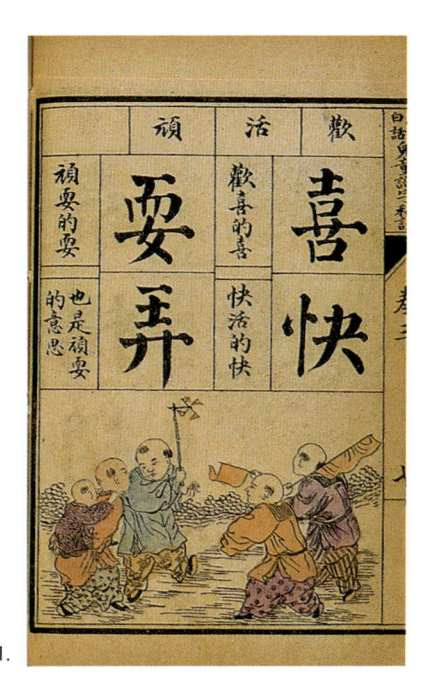

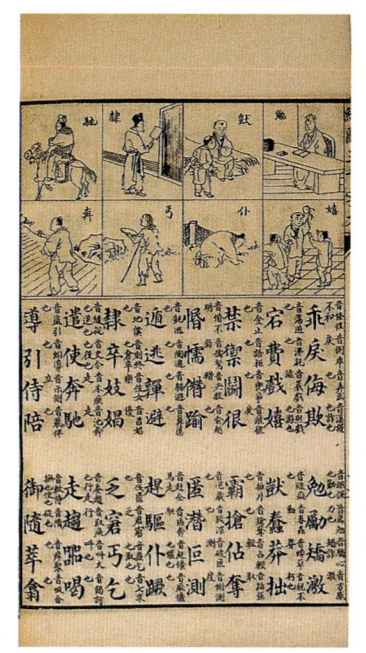

2.

1. ***Children's Secret Method of Chinese Character Recognition, Illustrated, in the Vernacular Language.* Guangyi Book Company, Shanghai, 1921.**
   Despite the fine illustrations, the "secret" method for learning to recognize characters is the tried and true method of rote learning. Three of the four characters on this page are "explained" by citing a two-character phrase in which the character appears. To give a rough example in English, to introduce the word "mobile," one would say, "mobile, as in automobile." The character in the upper left hand corner, *shua*, is explained: "like *shua* in the phrase *wan-shua*," which roughly translates as "play," as in "child's play," illustrated below. The fourth character, in the lower left hand corner, *nong*, is circuitously explained: "the same idea as *wan-shua*."

2. ***The Three Thousand Character Classic.* Wenyuan Book Company, no place, no date, *ca.* 1915.**
   A variation on the *Thousand Character Classic* in the form of a glossary of words arranged in groups of four. Some of the four-character phrases are full sentences, others are mere lists or synonyms. Each character is accompanied by a homonym to indicate pronunciation, followed by a synonym or brief definition, usually limited to two characters. The characters in the pictures in the top section of this page are, from right to left: (upper) *ride, official servant, silent, industrious*; (lower) *urgency, beg, fall prostrate, play*.

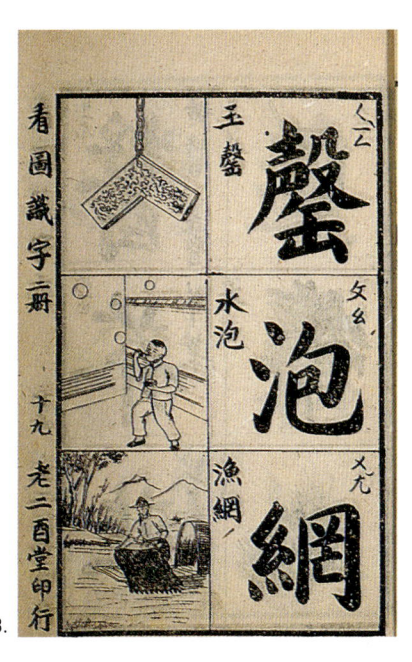

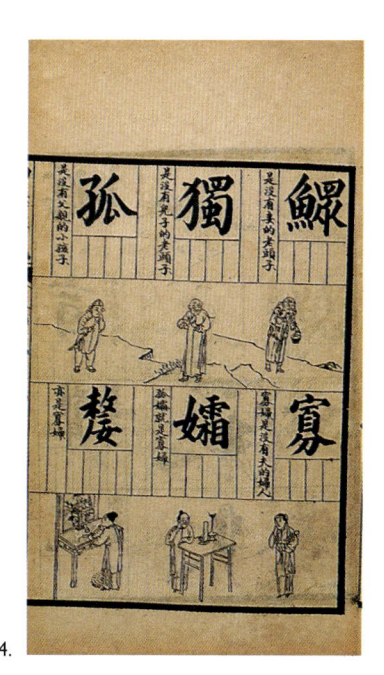

3.

4.

3. ***Character Recognition Through Pictures.* Published by Laoeryoutang, Beijing, no date, *ca.* 1930.**
   A traditional illustrated glossary that gives the pronunciation with tone marks in the upper right hand corner of the character frame, and to the left of the character a phrase in which it is used.

   Top: *Chime, jade chime.*   Middle: *Bubble, water bubble.*   Bottom: *Net, fishing net.*

4. ***Recognizing Chinese Characters is Really Easy! Volume 8.* Huihuitang and Shixuezhai, Hangzhou, no date, *ca.* 1915.**
   An illustrated thesaurus or glossary consisting of 18 volumes.

   Upper left to upper right: *orphan, man without offspring, widower.*   Lower right to lower left: *three terms for "widow."*

Early Pictorial Material

Gameboards for playing with dice
The Chinese were playing gambling games with dice as early as the Sui and Tang dynasties (581–907). By the Song dynasty (960–1279), with the rapid spread of printing, board games played with dice became popular. Using six dice, two players would advance or retreat around the track on the board according to the difference in the sums of their dice throws. The goal was to reach the center sqare. It is possible that such games as these, played by children at the New Year, influenced the *sugoroku* board games of Japan, also popular at the New Year, although scholars trace the origin of *sugoroku* to Buddhist pilgrimage diagrams that may have originated in the mandala, a symmetrical design used in Buddhist meditation.

Sheng guan tu **(official pecking order game). Qing dynasty, no date.**
By throwing dice and moving their pieces around the board from the outside towards the center, players progress through the ranks of officials, which here include prime minister, minister, district magistrate, scholar of the Hanlin Academy, Grand Examiner, and the first-ranking examinees in various stages in the imperial examination system.

Sheng guan tu **(official pecking order game). Qing dynasty, no date.**
The figures illustrated in the game are characters in the imaginary historical novel *Investiture of the Spirits (Fengshen yanyi)*, the cast of which consists of historical and mythological figures. As in the other game on this page, the object is to reach the central square first.

Early Pictorial Material

***Big Picture Reference Book*, 4 volumes. Science Bookstore and Guangxue Hui, Shanghai, 1908.**
An encyclopedia of drawings of people, plants, tools, clothing, housewares, etc. published in Shanghai three years before the end of the Qing dynasty. This picture, drawn from the section "Human Figures: Encouraging Study," shows a classroom setting with a Japanese or Western influence.

Cigarette cards for learning Chinese and English. No publisher, no date, *ca.* 1920.
Cigarette cards were introduced into China by foreign tobacco companies in the early 20th century. Typically, they were issued in sets, one card per pack of cigarettes, and were actively collected by children. Chinese cigarette cards were printed in a rich variety of striking designs, mostly with local content.

Early Pictorial Material

1.   2.   3.   4.

Cigarette cards: children's educational pictures. Hwaching Tobacco Co. Ltd., Shanghai, no date, *ca.* 1920.
From an unnumbered set of 24 cards produced by the Hwaching Tobacco Co.

1. Welcoming a guest
2. At the beginning of the school term, students bow to their teacher when they enter the schoolyard
3. Doing homework by the light of an oil lamp
4. Cleaning the classroom

1.   2.   3.

4.   5.   6.

Tangram cards. Distributed by the Shanghai branch of the Xinhua Bookstore. No date, *ca.* 1950.
The tangram puzzle, in which seven small pieces of wood or paper are combined to form familiar shapes, spread to Europe from China in the early 19th century and has been popular ever since. The date of its origin in China is under dispute, but geometric construction puzzles like the tangram were known in the Song dynasty (960–1279). Similar in format to cigarette cards, these tangram cards were a commercial product, as indicated on the card with the bathing boy, which gives the price.

1. Playing the piano
2. Torch
3. Bathing
4. Barber chair
5. Peach

Early Pictorial Material

Cigarette cards: traditional Chinese professions. Pinhead Cigarettes, no date, *ca.* 1920.

1. *Cleaning out portable toilets*
2. *Dealer in rare furs*
3. *Plate-spinning acrobat*
4. *Peddler of bows*
5. *Shoeing a horse*
6. *Making toys out of melted sugar*
7. *Lion dancers*
8. *Basket repairman*
9. *Clock repairman*

1910s–1920s

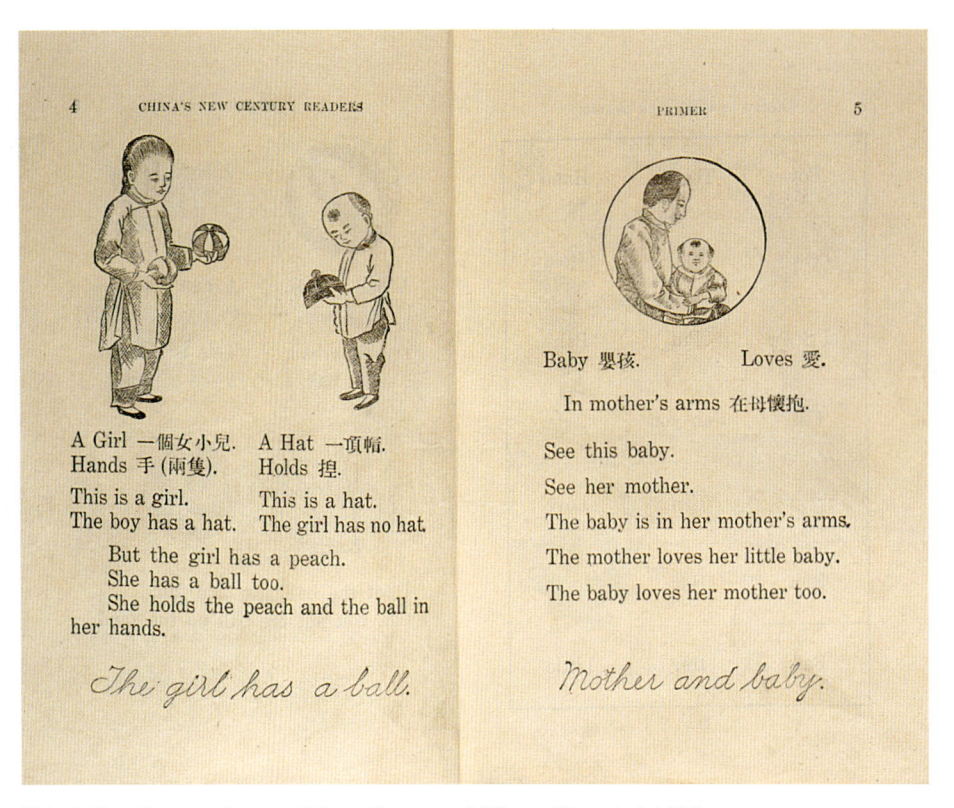

China's New Century Readers: Primer. Commercial Press, Shanghai, 1914.
Founded in 1897, the Commercial Press in Shanghai has remained one of the most influential publishing houses in China.

An untitled advertising circular for children's textbooks. Commercial Press, Shanghai, no date, *ca*. 1925.

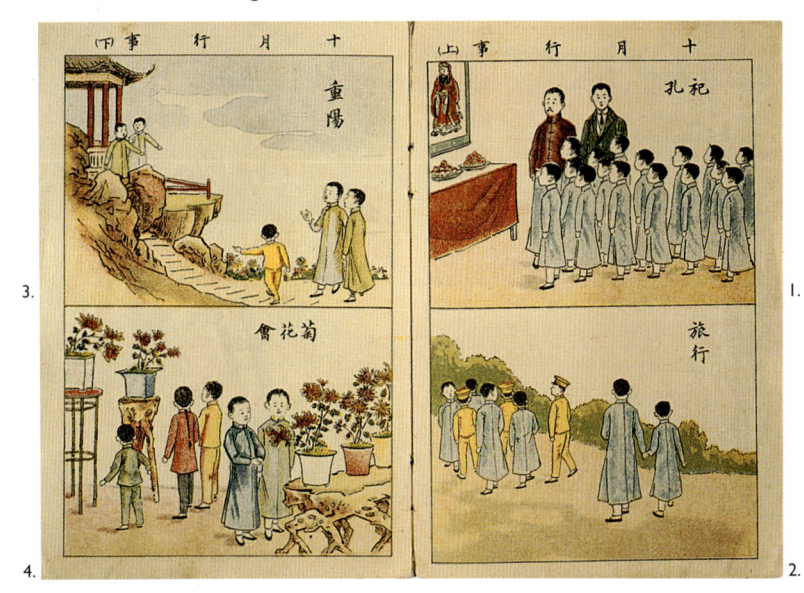

October Activities
1. Performing a ritual in honor of Confucius
2. An outing
3. The Double Ninth Festival (ninth day of the ninth lunar month)
4. Chrysanthemum exhibition

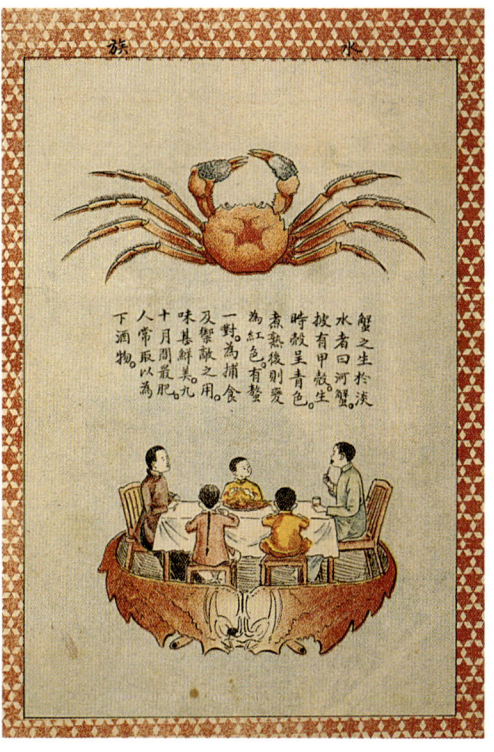

Crabs that live in fresh water are called "river crabs." They have hard shells. When alive, their shells are a blue-green color. When they are cooked, the shell turns red. Crabs have a pair of pincers used for capturing their prey and for self defense. They are delicious to eat. Their flesh is plentiful and tender in the months of September and October. Rice wine is a common accompaniment to crabs.

1910s–1920s

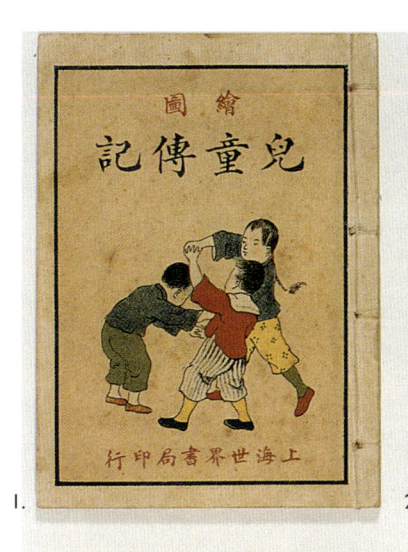

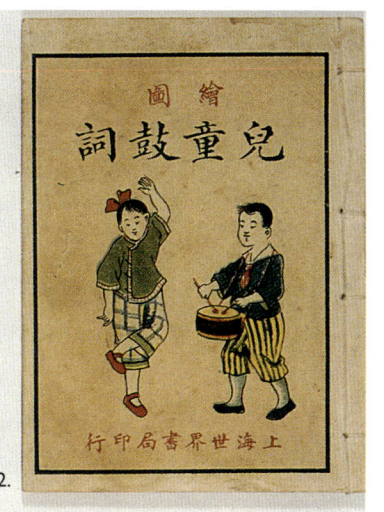

Children's Amusement Park. World Book Company, Shanghai, 1925.
A boxed series of 14 miniature books, string-bound in traditional fashion. Contents include biographies of famous people, riddles, composition practice, jokes, poetry, arts and crafts and games. In some volumes, the cover illustration is not related to the contents.

1. *Biographies of Famous People for Children*
2. *"Drum Songs" (simple poems) for Children*
3. *Jokes for Children*
4. *Composition for Children*

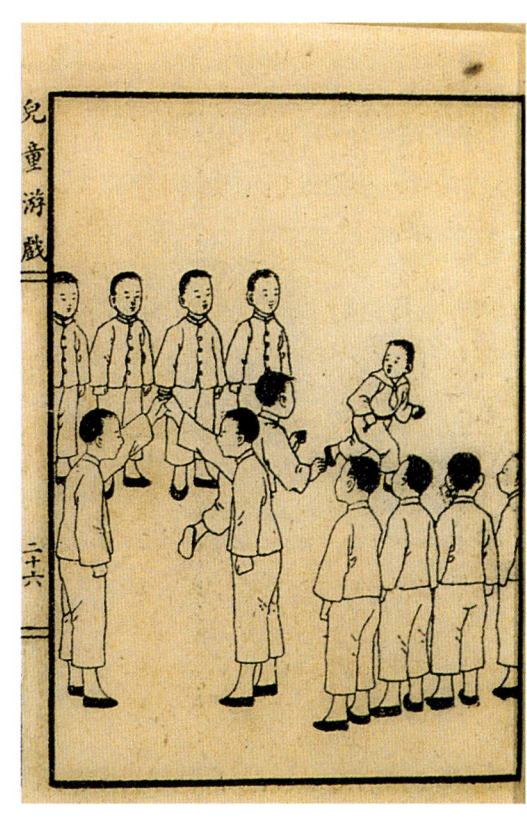

From *Games for Children*
Viewed from a distance, the children look like a memorial archway.

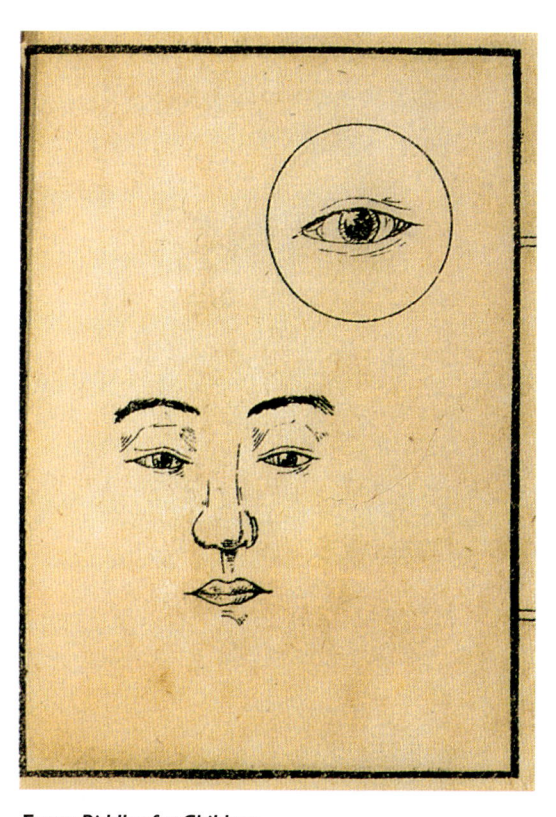

From *Riddles for Children*
Two sisters are separated by a wall; but through their entire lives they never meet face to face.

1910s–1920s

Children's World magazine
First published in Shanghai by the Commercial Press in 1922, under the editorship of the scholar Zheng Zhenduo.

Cover of *Children's World* magazine. June 16, 1923.

***The Candle Disaster*, by Guo Qingchang**

Father is painting.
When Junior leans forward to get a closer look at what his father is doing, his hair catches fire.
When father turns to look at Junior's hair, his beard catches fire.

Cover of *Children's World* magazine. April 1, 1927

Cover of *Children's World* magazine. November 20, 1926

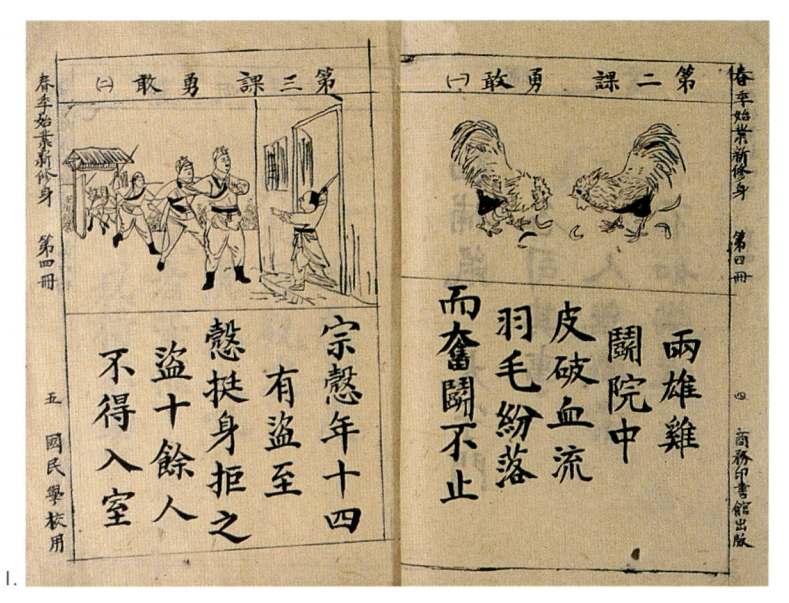

1910s–1920s

1. **A manuscript copy of a Republican textbook, *New Ethics, Spring Term,* for Beginning Students, for Use in Public Schools. No date, ca. 1915.**
   Possibly the work of an entrepreneurial scribe or teacher, the existence of this book suggests that textbooks were either expensive or unavailable in certain parts of China. Although copyrights were reserved for these textbooks, the copier faithfully wrote the name of the publisher, Commercial Press, on the margin of every page.

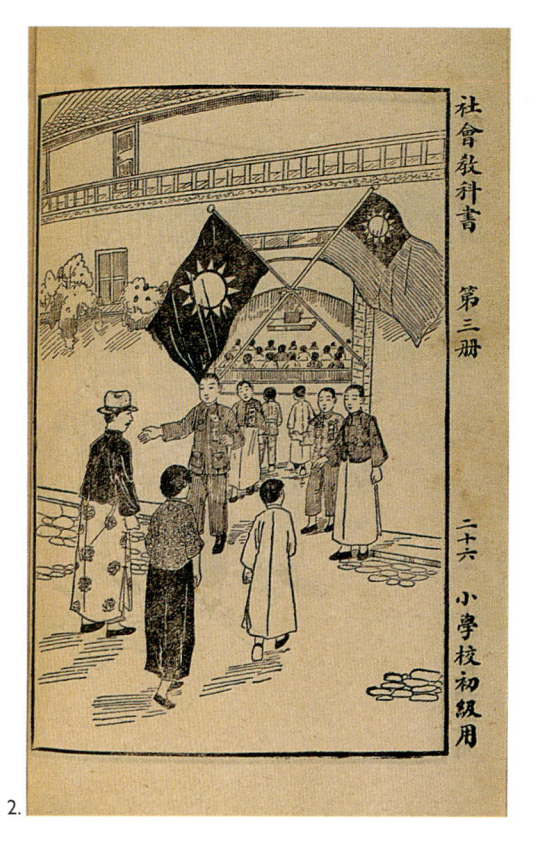

2. ***New Age Social Studies Textbook,* for Lower Primary Schools, Volume 3. Commercial Press, Shanghai, 1927.**
   The dress of the figures includes the long gown, jacket and long gown and the Sun Yat-sen jacket, with four pockets, later known as the Mao jacket.

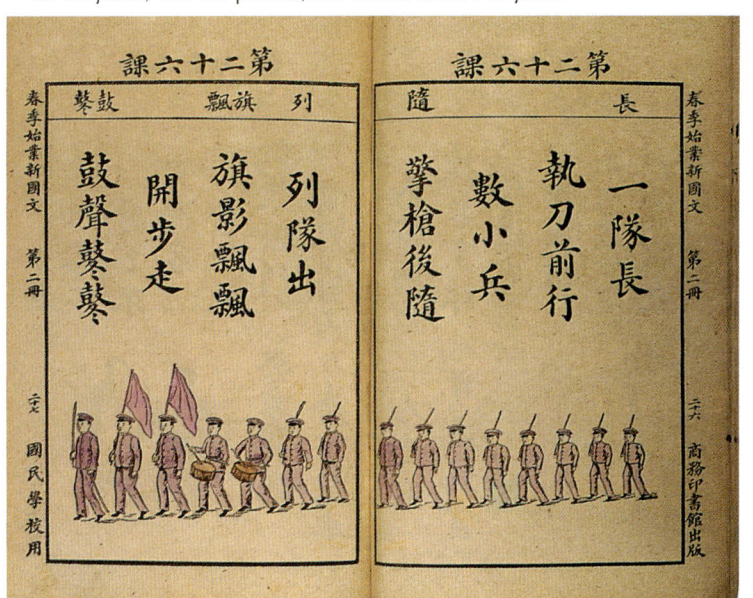

3. ***Republican Series, National Readers,* for Lower Primary Schools, for Two Semesters, Approved by the Board of Education. Volume 2. Commercial Press, Shanghai, 1912.**

   The drill team leader, carrying a sword, marches forward. Behind him, several little soldiers holding rifles follow in step. The drill team marches on, their flags fluttering in the sun. As they step ahead, their drums sound "dong dong."

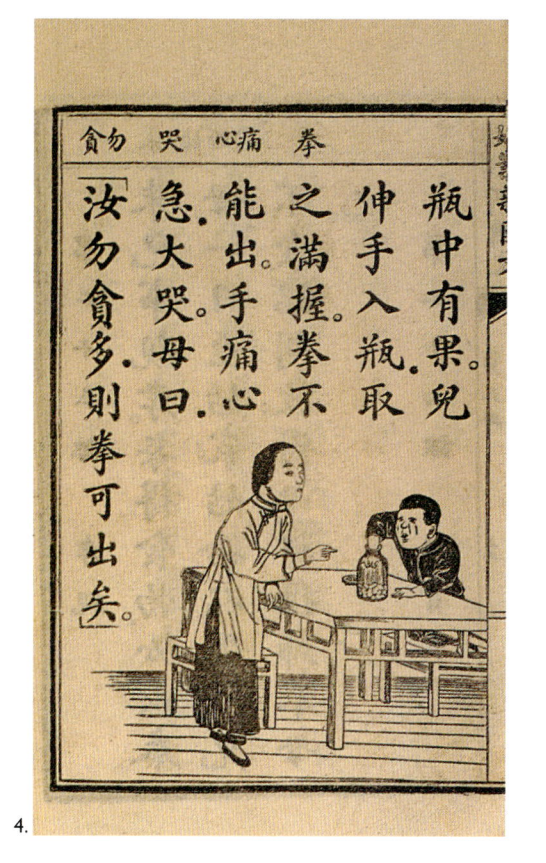

4. ***Republican Series, National Readers,* for Lower Primary Schools, for Two Semesters, Approved by the Board of Education, Volume 3. Commercial Press, Shanghai, 1922.**
   Reprint of a popular textbook first published in the first year of the Republic (1912), in the literary language.

   There is candy in the jar. The boy sticks his hand into the jar. He grabs a fistful of candy, but having made a fist, he cannot extract his hand from the jar. His hand hurts, and in a panic he starts to cry. His mother says: "Don't be so greedy. If you take less candy, you can remove your hand from the jar."

31

1910s–1920s

New Ideology Civics Text, for Lower Primary School, Volume 1. World Book Company, Shanghai, 1927.

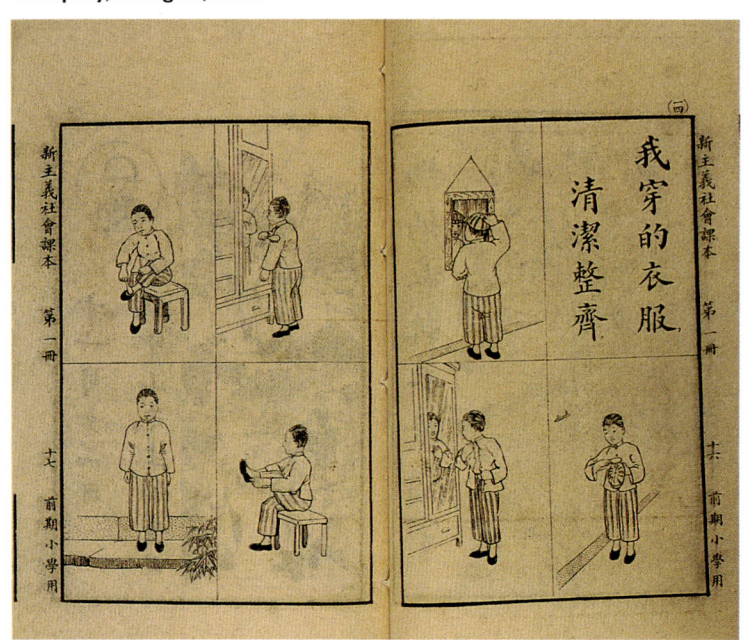

The clothing I wear is neat and clean.

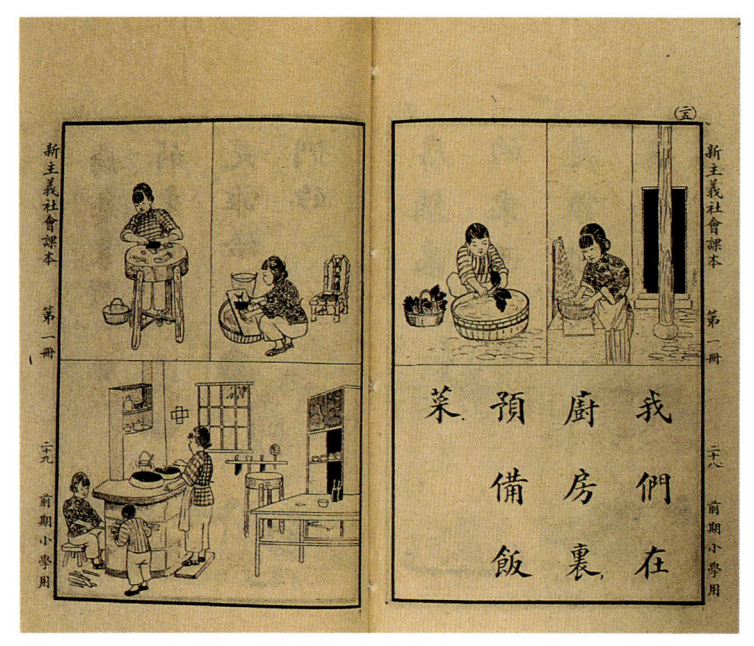

We prepare a meal of rice and fried dishes in the kitchen.

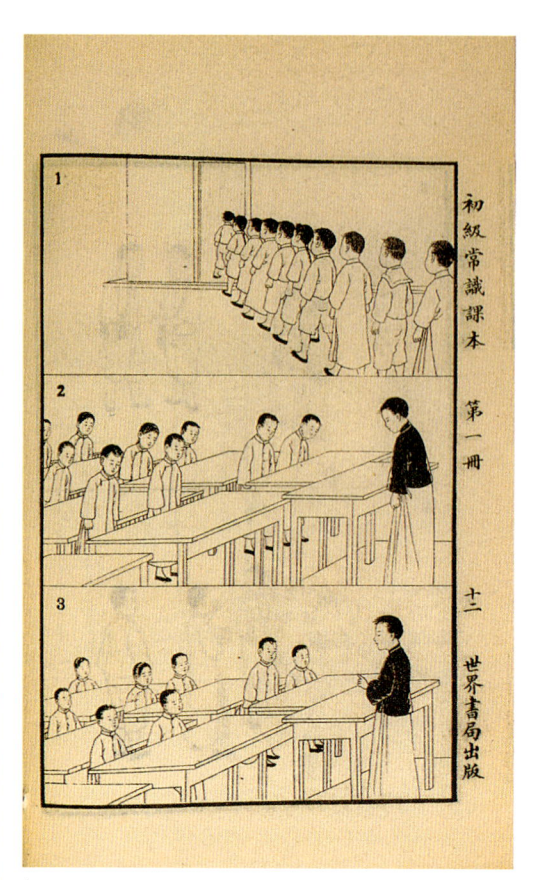

1. *Useful Knowledge Series (Illustrated), Specially Compiled under the New System, for the Use of Lower Primary Schools, Volume 1.* World Book Company, Shanghai, 1924.
   Pictures for class discussion, no text. The topic of the pictures is classroom decorum and discipline.

   The school bell has rung!

2. *Useful Knowledge Series (Illustrated), Specially Compiled under the New System, for the Use of Lower Primary Schools, Volume 2.* World Book Company, Shanghai, 1924.
   Shop exterior and interior, an illustration for class discussion.

1910s–1920s

Beginning Religion Textbook, for Primary School, Volume I. Northern Fujian Catholic Book Association, Fuzhou, 1930.

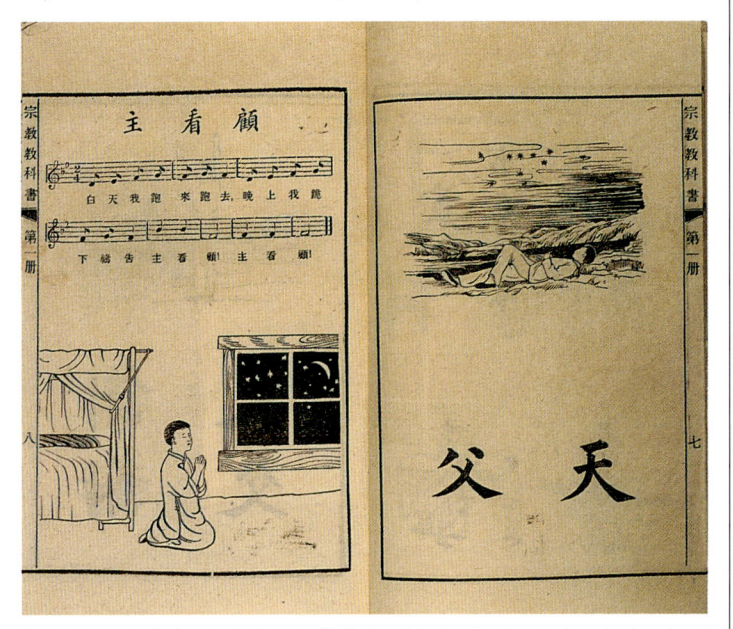

Right: *Heavenly Father.* Left: *"Under God's Care" In the day I rush about In the night I kneel down to pray.*

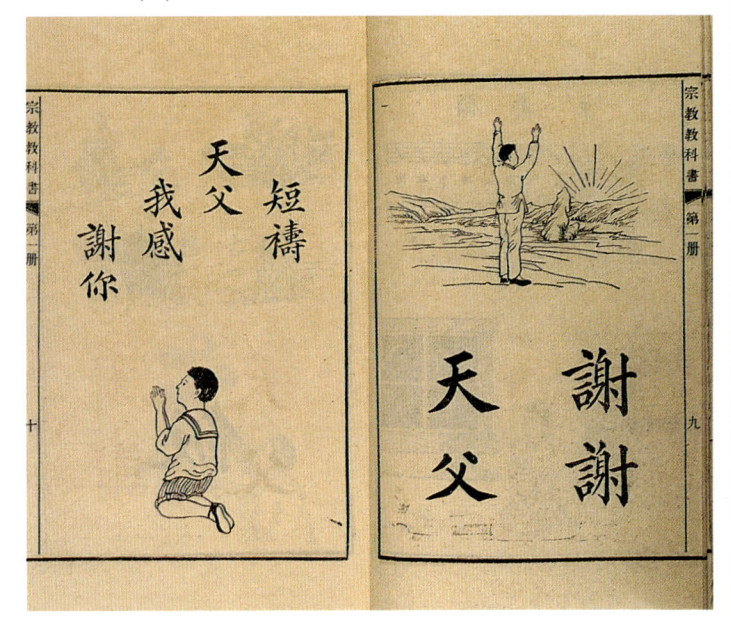

Right: *Thank you, Heavenly Father*
Left: *Short Prayer: Father in Heaven, I thank you*

The texts relating to the illustrations on the right read:

1. *Human Models*
   In the window of the Huaying Pharmacy, Fang Huasheng and his older sister see a human skeleton and a human body. The eyes, ears, mouth and nose of the human body all appear normal, but the stomach, liver, intestines and lungs are exposed. Huasheng says to his sister: "These two things are terrifying! What are they used for?" His sister replies: "There is no reason to be scared of them! These are two human models that can teach you about the structure of the human body."

2. *China's National Shame*
   The Chinese people have much experience avenging insults. Thus whenever they hear the tale of how the King of Yue [Gou Jian] nursed his vengeance ("lay on a straw bed and tasted gall") to wipe out a humiliation he suffered at the hands of the King of Wu [whom he eventually defeated], they are visibly overjoyed ("eyebrows flying, face dancing"). However, in the past several decades, China has lost territory to foreigners, has paid indemnities, has surrendered her sovereign rights and suffered other acts of national humiliation. How can one compare what befell the King of Yue to China's recent national humiliation? As citizens of China, what can we do?

Textbook of One Thousand Characters for Townspeople. Published for the Chinese National Association of Mass Education Movement. Commercial Press, Shanghai, 1927.

A much reprinted textbook "for the use of adults and youth" in the form of a series of lessons. The text on the facing page (not shown) is set vertically, with new vocabulary words introduced in the lesson picked out again in large characters below.

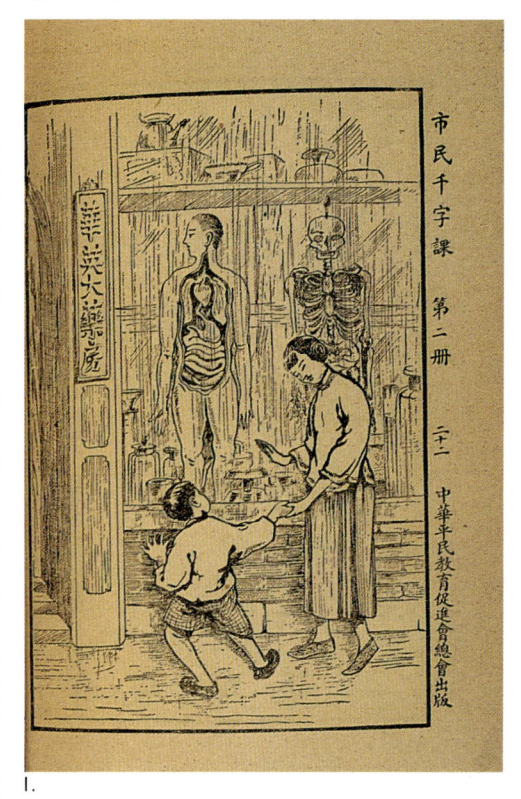

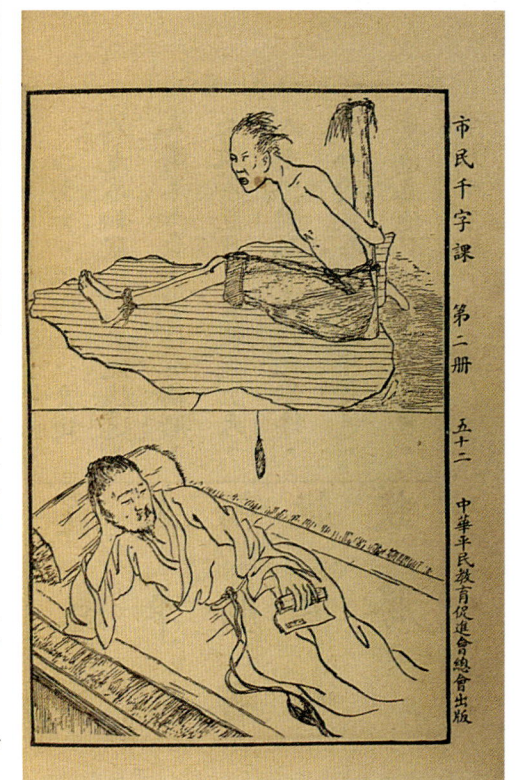

1.

2.

1930s

Little Rhymes, 2 volumes. **World Book Company, Shanghai, 1932.**

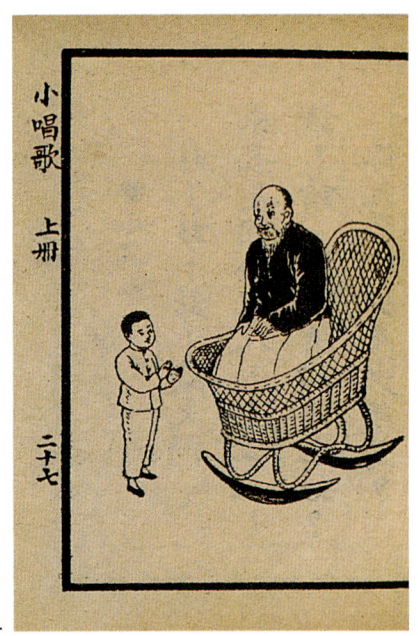

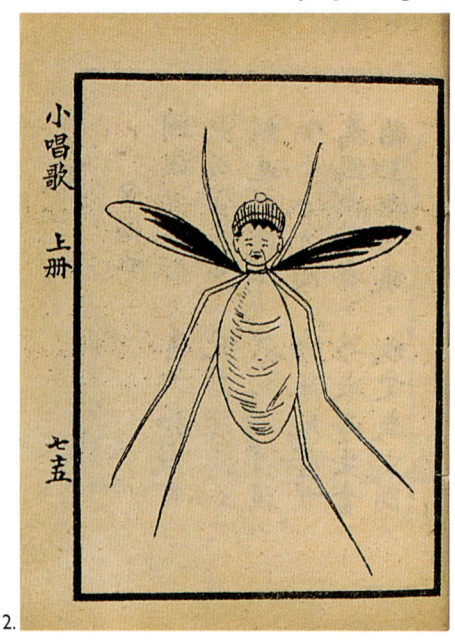

1. Really Strange
   Strange, strange, very very strange
   A sparrow tramples to death an old lady hen
   An ant grows to be three feet long
   An old man of 80 sits in a cradle

2. The mosquito cries weng weng
   The mosquito bites big brother,
   Big brother giggles heh heh
   The mosquito bites little brother
   Little brother laughs hee hee
   The mosquito bites the baby

   The baby smiles gently
   The mosquito bites aunty
   Aunty laughs ha ha
   The mosquito's drunk its belly full
   It cannot fly and cannot run
   It can only cry now, weng weng weng.

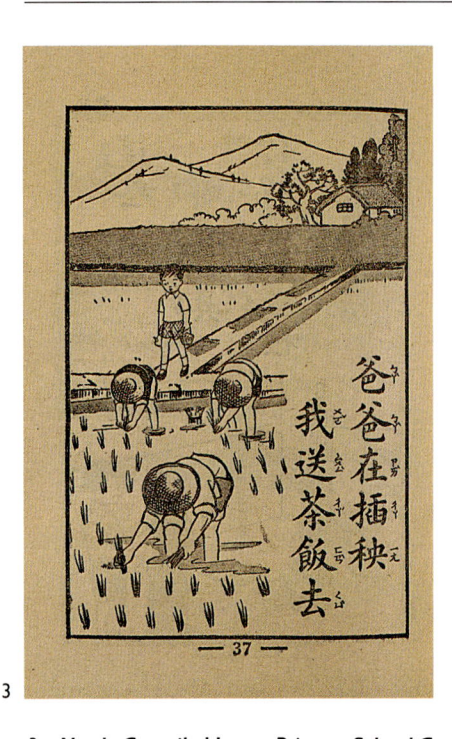

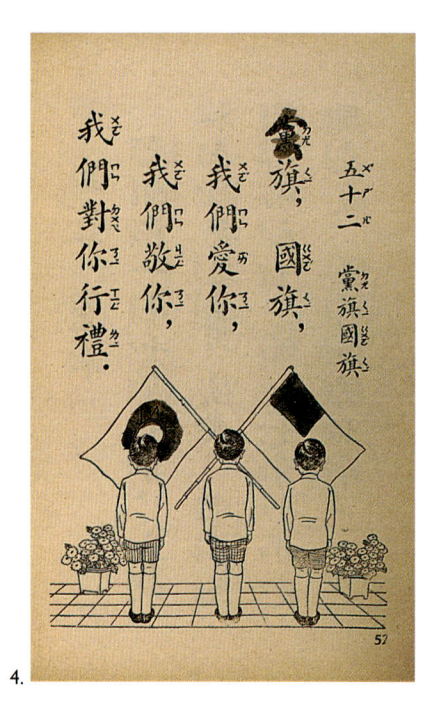

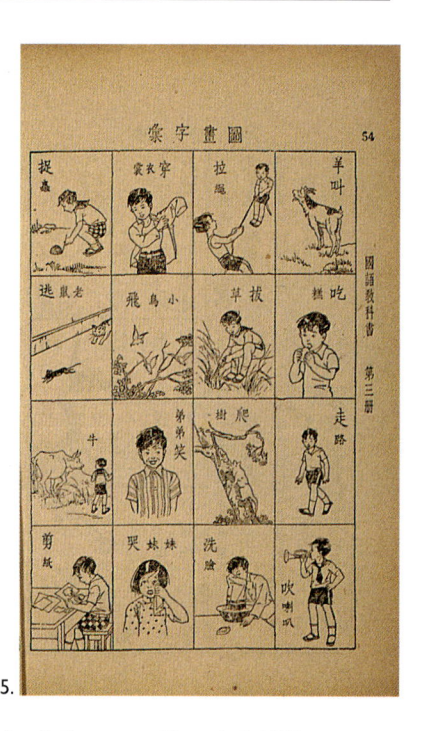

3. ***Newly Compiled Lower Primary School Common Knowledge Textbook,* Volume 2. Chung Hwa Book Company, Shanghai, 1939.**
   Father is planting rice seedlings. I bring him tea and food.

4. ***Short Term Primary School Textbook,* Volume 1, Revised edition. Edited by the National Textbook Compilation Bureau; distributed jointly by Commercial Press, Chung Hwa Book Company, World Book Company (all Shanghai) and Zhongzheng Book Company, Nanjing, 1936.**
   An example of a textbook complied by the Republican government during a short-lived experiment in centralized educational publishing.

   Lesson 52: The national flag and the party flag
   Oh, Party flag, Oh national flag: we love you, we respect you, we salute you.

   In the text, the word "party" is inked out, as are the stars on the KMT party flag (left) and national flag (right). A little bit of political correctness goes a long way: by inking out a few flags and the neutral word "party," the book was "liberated" for use as a learning tool.

5. ***Chinese Language Textbook, Lower Primary Schools,* Volume 3. Commercial Press, Shanghai, 1933. From a series of *Chinese Renaissance* textbooks.**
   Pictures to aid in character recognition. The entries on this page are mostly verb-noun combinations. Beginning in the upper left hand corner: *catching insects; getting dressed; pulling a rope; a goat bleats; a rat flees; a little bird flies; pulling weeds; eating cake...*

My Pictorial magazine, Volume 11. New China Book Company, Shanghai, May 15, 1933.

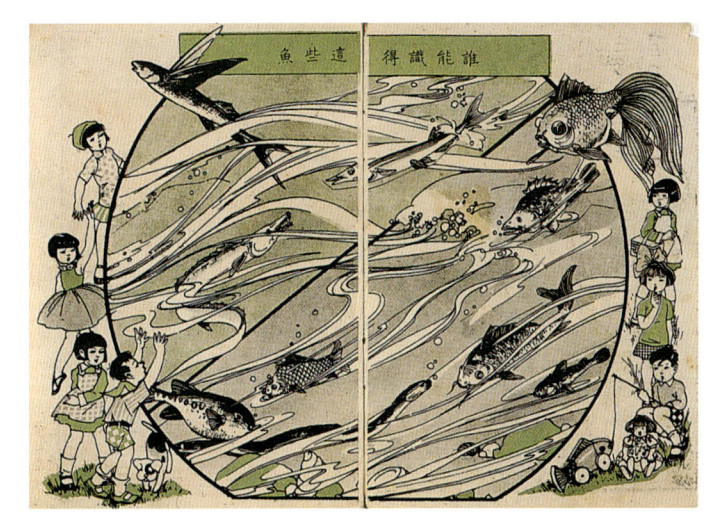

Who can identify the fish in this picture?

Acts of national humiliation that took place in May

Right : *Remember, remember, remember: May 9, 1915*
The slip of paper a Japanese official is handing to a Chinese says: "Twenty-one Demands" which included recognizing Japan's privileged position in Shandong, Manchuria and Inner Mongolia, Japan's right to jointly operate iron and steel industries in China as well as the right to control several key Chinese government bureaus. The president of the Republic of China, Yuan Shikai, accepted these demands with a few changes, which caused a national outcry.

Left : *Remember, remember, remember: Remember the national humiliation of May 3, 1928.*
On this day, vicious fighting broke out in Jinan, the capital of Shandong province, between Japanese troops and the northern expeditionary troops of Chiang Kai-shek. Japan had sent 5000 troops to Jinan to protect the 2000 Japanese civilians living there. Arriving in Jinan, Chiang asked the Japanese troops to withdraw, which they refused to do, and "...the skirmish grew into a devastating clash in which appalling atrocities, including castration and blinding of helpless prisoners, were committed by both sides." (Jonathan D. Spence, *The Search for Modern China*. W.W. Norton, New York, 1990.)

1.

2.

1. **An advertising pamphlet published by the Xinyi Medicine Company in Shanghai, 1940.**
The pamphlet contains several dozen amusing and edifying stories of child prodigies.

Wang Pangyou
In the Song dynasty, there lived a clever boy called Wang Pangyou. When he was six, he accompanied one of his father's friends to the zoo, where they saw a cage containing two animals. The gentleman asked young Wang, "One of these animals is a river deer, the other is a deer. Can you tell them apart?"

Wang replied, "The animal next to the river deer is a deer, and the animal next to the deer is the river deer."

Actually, Wang had never seen either of those animals before. For a six-year-old child to be able to answer that question so cleverly is admirable. Such a question would certainly baffle most adults.

2. ***Nature Study for Primary School, For the New Standard Curriculum, Volume 1.* Chung Hwa Book Company, 1933.**

Tonight the moon is beautiful.

1930s

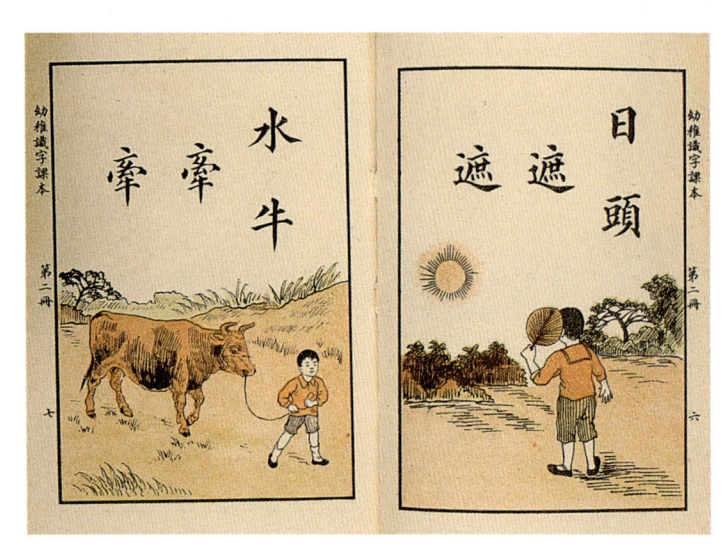

Chinese Character Recognition for Toddlers. Guangyi Bookstore, Shanghai, 1935.

Right: *Sun; shade oneself, shade oneself*
Left: *Water buffalo; pull, pull*

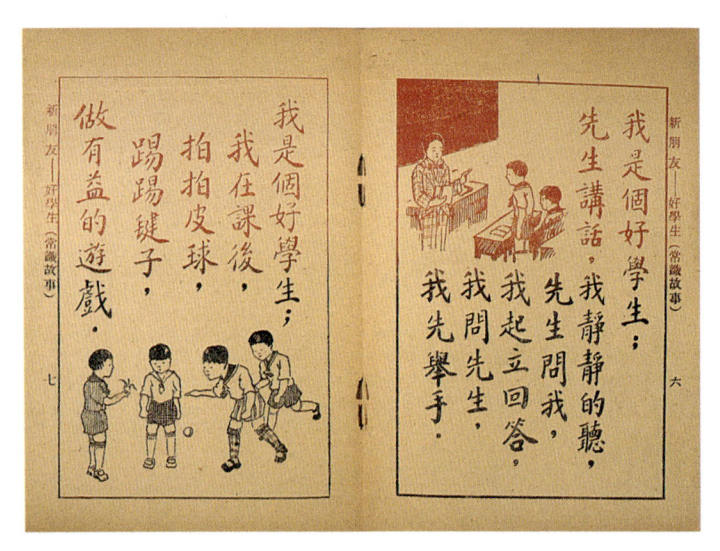

New Friends—Good Student, An Elementary Reader. Children's Bookstore, Shanghai, 1931.

Right: *I am a good student: When the teacher is talking, I listen quietly. When the teacher asks me a question, I stand up to answer him. When I ask the teacher a question, I first raise my hand.*
Left: *I am a good student: After class, I play ball and kick the shuttlecock, both beneficial games.*

Children's Graphic Magazine. Commercial Press, Shanghai, July 5, 1937.

How the Brain Works
The human brain can be compared to a machine. Each part of the brain is in charge of a different activity. Some parts control speech, others are responsible for sight, movement [of the hands and feet] and hearing (as well as balance, thought, smell, taste and touch).

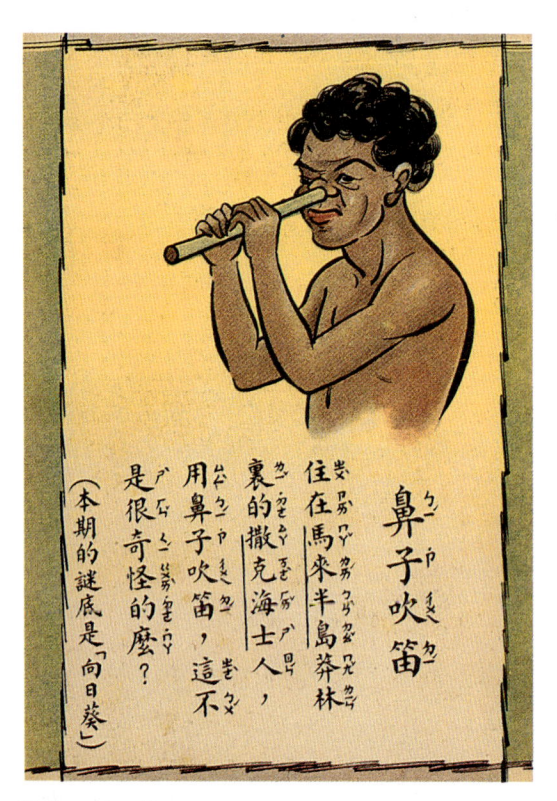

Playing a Nose Flute
The Sakehaishi [sic] people who live on the Malay Peninsula play a type of flute with their noses. Isn't that strange?

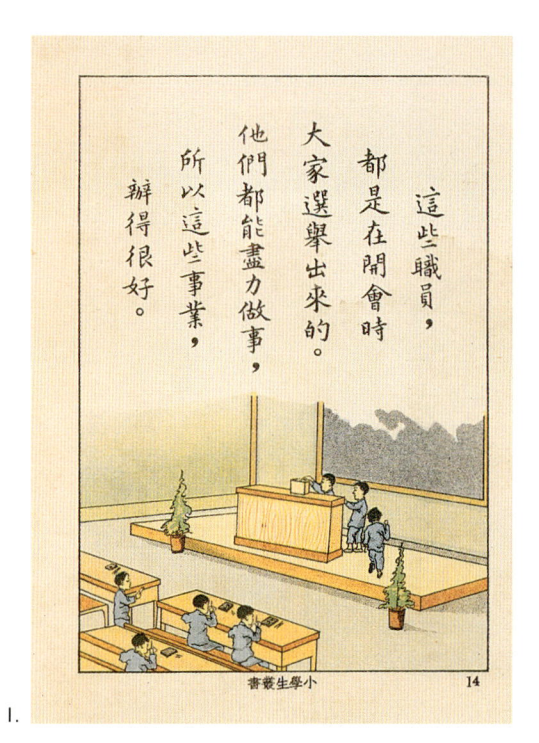

1. ***A Village School. From the series, Primary School Student's Collection.*** **Chung Hwa Book Company, Shanghai, 1931.**
These officers [of a student organization], were elected to office by all the members of the organization during a meeting. They will work very hard, and thus all the necessary tasks will be carried out satisfactorily.

2. ***Tiny Pictorial.*** **Children's Bookstore, Shanghai, October 1, 1936.**
Society: Exposition of What Children Eat All Over the World by Lin Jiasheng.

Upper left–upper right:
Japanese children eat fish.
European and American children eat bread.
Chinese children:
In Mongolia they drink goat's milk.
In North China they eat noodles.
In South China they eat rice.

Lower left–lower right:
Children in Africa eat sweet potatoes.
Children in the North Pole eat bear meat.
Children in Malaysia eat coconut.

3. ***Hot Places, A Supplementary Geography Reader for Young Children.*** **Shihuan Publishing Company, Shanghai, 1933.**
The covers of this and the next book, by Shen Yingquan, show the influence of constructivism.

4. ***Mr. Water, A Supplementary Nature Reader for Young Children.*** **Shihuan Publishing Company, Shanghai, 1933.**

1930s

Children's Graphic Magazine. Commercial Press, Shanghai, August 5, 1935.

Giant steps around the maypole

Children's Graphic Magazine. **Commercial Press, Shanghai, May 20, 1937.**
In the Cotsen Children's Library copy of this magazine, the Kuomintang (KMT) insignia on the wings and tail of the airplane have been inked out by hand, a graphic representation of partisanship in a time of national crisis.

Parachuting Demonstration.

Children's Graphic Magazine. **Commercial Press, Shanghai, September 16, 1933.**

Wild Geese and Soldiers: A formation of wild geese in the sky, a platoon of soldiers on the ground. Although their destinations differ, they are all moving forward.

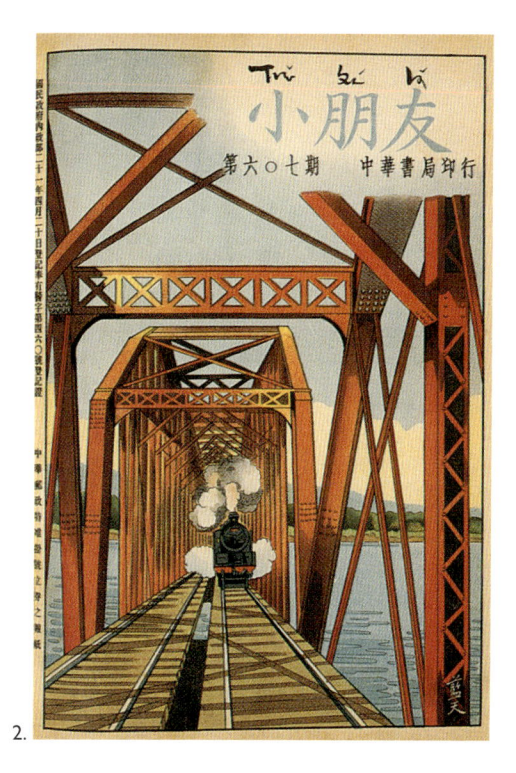

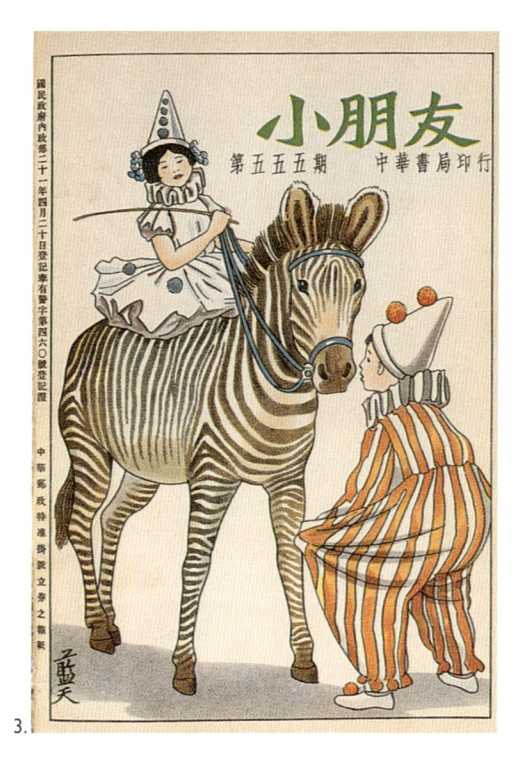

1. ***Children's Graphic* magazine. Commercial Press, Shanghai, May 20, 1937.**
   The boy soldier's call to arms is an accurate reflection of China on the verge of war. Japan had occupied Manchuria since 1931. The Xi'an Incident, resulting in nationalist and communist troops agreeing to cooperate against the Japanese, had taken place in December 1936. Six weeks after the publication date of this magazine, on July 7, 1937, Japanese soldiers outside Beijing provoked a skirmish with Chinese soldiers that led within days to China's embroilment in World War II.

2. ***Xiao pengyou* magazine. Commercial Press, Shanghai. March 14, 1937; June 15, 1933; August 3, 1933.**
   Three covers by Lan Tian.
   Initially published by the Chung Hwa Bookstore, *Xiao pengyou* is one of the earliest and longest-running magazines in China. The inaugural issue, in the Cotsen Children's Library, dates from April 1922. The magazine stopped publication during the Japanese occupation (1939–45) and again during the Cultural Revolution (1966–78), and has undergone several changes in publisher and target audience. In recent years, circulation has reached 1.1 million copies.

3. *Xiao pengyou* magazine, June 15, 1933.

4. *Xiao pengyou* magazine, August 3, 1933.

Japanese Occupation

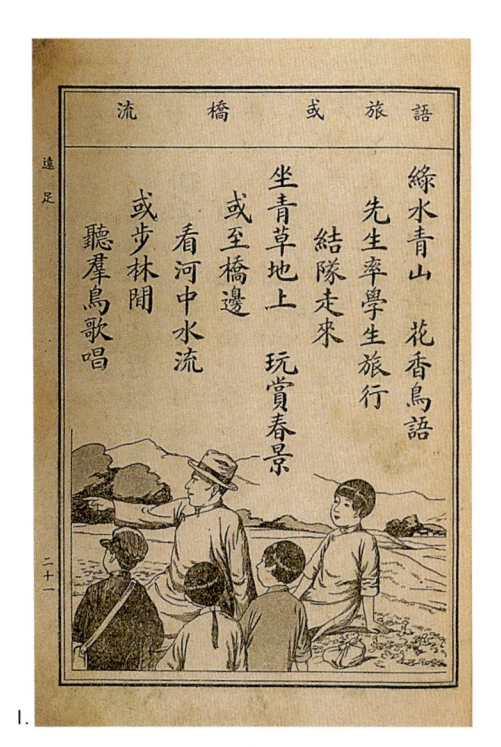

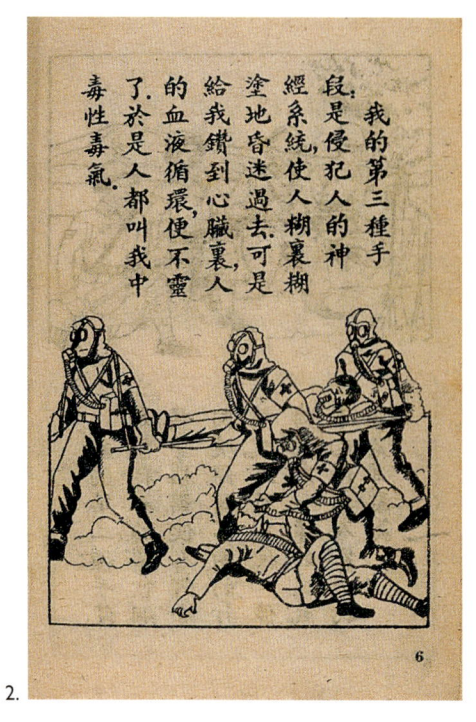

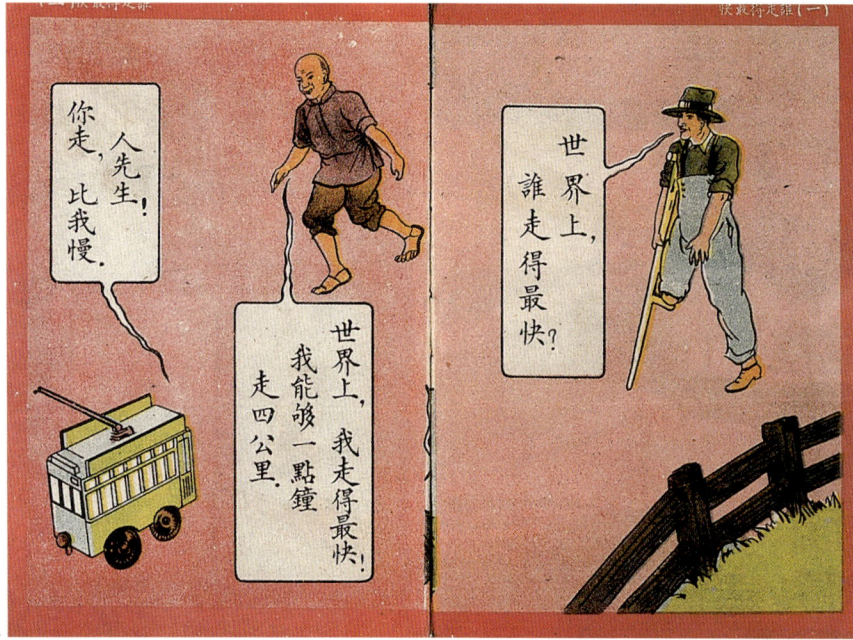

1. **Chinese Language Textbook for Public Schools, Volume 3. Dated the 735th year of Genghis (Chinggis) Khan, probably 1941.**
   Written and distributed by the Department of Civil Administration, then under Japanese control. Printed by the Manchukuo Book Corporation, Xinjing (Changchun) during the Manchukuo period. Price is given in Mongolian currency.

   A Hike: After the spring rains, when the willow catkins fill the air, and the scenery in the countryside gradually turns fine—there are indigo streams and emerald hills, fragrant flowers and singing birds—the teacher takes several students on an outing. The students walk in a line. Some sit on the grass and enjoy the spring vistas, some stand on a bridge and watch the water flowing in the stream, while others walk in the woods and listen to the singing birds.

2. **The Autobiography of Poison Gas. Dalu Book Company, Xinjing (Changchun), 1943.**
   One of a series of "autobiographies" of inventions, industries and scientific processes, written in the first person. The date is given as the "ninth year of Kangde," the reign title adopted by the last Chinese emperor, Puyi, when he was made emperor of Manchukuo in 1934.

   My third modus operandi: I attack the human nervous system, forcing people into a state of mental confusion. Within minutes, they pass out. When I work my way into the heart, I can seriously disturb the circulatory system. In this manifestation, people call me "poison gas."

3. **Stories For Young Children. Dalu Book Company, Xinjing (Changchun), 1944.**
   One of a series of illustrated books published in Changchun, then called Xinjing (New Capital), the capital of the Japanese puppet-state Manchukuo. Dated 1944, "the tenth year of Kangde," the reign title given to Puyi, which began in March 1934.

   [Man with crutch]: *Who in the world walks the fastest?*
   [Man in sandals]: *I am the fastest walker in the world. In one hour I can cover four kilometers.*
   [Trolley Bus]: *Gentlemen! No matter how fast you walk, you are slower than I am!*

Japanese Occupation

New Youth magazine, published in Beijing 1940–45 by the New Youth Magazine Press.
An overtly pro-Japanese boys' magazine published during the Japanese occupation of Beijing, it appear to be modeled after the highly successful Japanese magazine, *Shonen Club*, which flourished in Japan at this time. A publisher's notation reads: "the mission of this magazine is to use the impetus of culture to nourish youth to become the core members in the movement for the Asian renaissance."

New Youth magazine, July 1944.
The cover shows a soldier guarding the ruins of the Yuanmingyuan Garden in Beijing, a symbol of Chinese culture under foreign assault. Fighter planes dot the sky. The five characters at the lower right hand corner of the page read: "Protect the Great East Asia Co-Prosperity Sphere," Japan's empire in Asia.

New Youth magazine, November 1943.

New Youth magazine, December 1943.

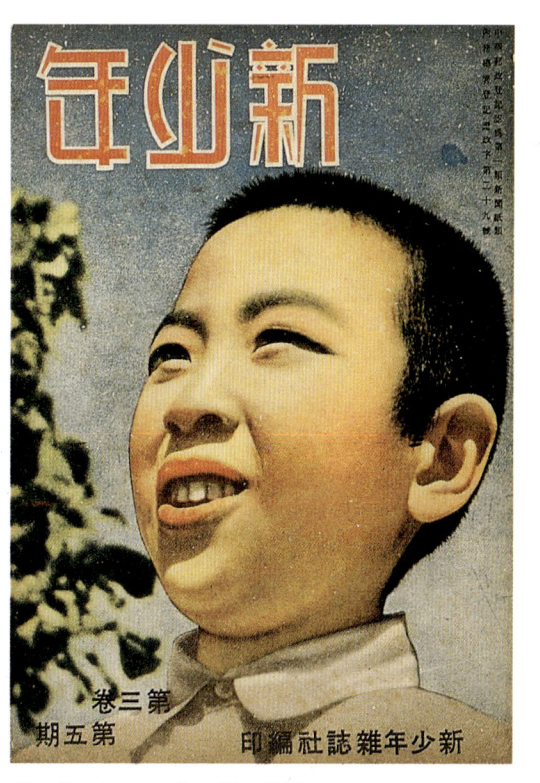

New Youth magazine, May 1943.

1940s

Model Diary Entries for Children, Volume 3. Children's Book Company, Shanghai, 1947.

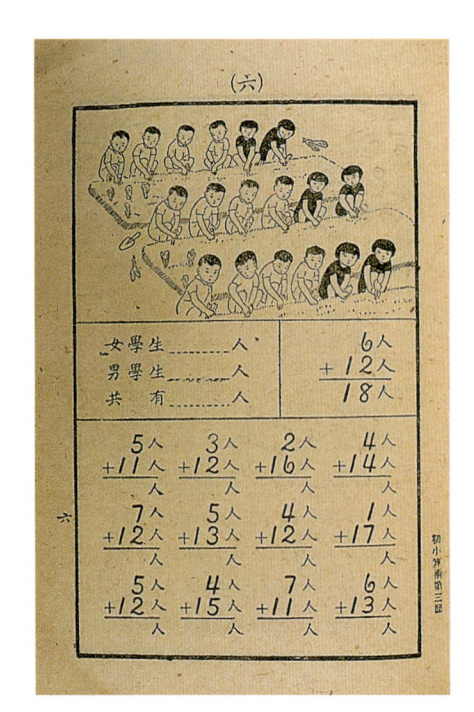

Lower Primary School Arithmetic, Volume 3. National Textbook Compilation Bureau, distributed by World Book Company, Shanghai, 1947.

Killing bedbugs with DDT
Sunday, 16 May. Clear 75 degrees, Fahrenheit
The text (not shown) reads:
As the days grew warmer, the bedbugs grew more lively. This made Mother very upset. She would wake up in the middle of the night, scratching her bedbug bites. But the itching never went away.

    Today father went out and bought some DDT. When he brought it home, we sprayed it everywhere: on the ceiling, floor, windows, tables, closets and even in the toilet. ...

    I was afraid that DDT would ruin the curtains, but Father said: "No, it won't. You can spray DDT on your skin, or on vegetables, and it won't do any harm. As long as you don't swallow it, it's not at all dangerous..."

    Science is truly progressing in leaps and bounds. I hope scientists will invent more kinds of insecticide, rather than create weapons that can kill people.

1. ***Children's Knowledge 14.*** Children's Book Company, Shanghai, August 1947.
   A series of colorful monthly publications for very young readers, published in Shanghai by the Children's Book Company from 1946 for at least two years.

2. ***Children's Knowledge 23.*** Children's Book Company, Shanghai, May 1948.

1940s

Children's Knowledge 15. **Children's Book Company, Shanghai, September 1947.**

Comic Strip by Feng Zikai
1. Man kills a chicken.
2. Chicken kills a spider.
3. Spider kills a fly.
4. Flies kill people.

(Right) *Children's Knowledge 19.* **Children's Book Company, Shanghai, December 1947.**

Comic Strip by Feng Zikai
1. I have two bills here, just enough to buy two persimmons.
2. Look at this poor old beggar! I'll give him one bill.
3. What a sad-looking young beggar. I'll give him the other bill.
4. Two persimmons fall off the tree!

(Below) *Children's Knowledge,* Volume 4. Children's Book Company, Shanghai. (1946–48)
A patriotic, anti-Nationalist reader has crossed out the illustrations of the Nationalist flag and of Generalissimo Chiang Kai-shek shaking hands with an unidentifiable Western man. The lyrics of the song, "The Chrysanthemums are Yellow," are by He Qing.

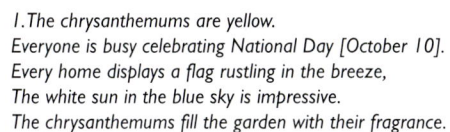

1. The chrysanthemums are yellow.
Everyone is busy celebrating National Day [October 10].
Every home displays a flag rustling in the breeze,
The white sun in the blue sky is impressive.
The chrysanthemums fill the garden with their fragrance.

2. The chrysanthemums are yellow.
Everyone is busy carrying out national construction,
A task even more daunting than defeating the Japanese.
Yet we will undertake any difficulty,
Chrysanthemums never wither in the frost.

3. The chrysanthemums are yellow.
Because we are busy studying,
We try to master knowledge and skills,
No one helps us, we help ourselves.
The chrysanthemum stands alone in the glory of autumn.

4. The chrysanthemums are yellow.
The world is trying to end all wars.
China is already a first-class nation,
We should take this responsibility upon ourselves.
The chrysanthemum was originally the flower of peace.

1940s

Three covers from *Primary School Student Semi-Monthly*, Primary School Student Publishing Company, Shanghai.

Primary School Student, November 1, 1944.

Primary School Student, February 1, 1945.

Primary School Student, August 1, 1944.

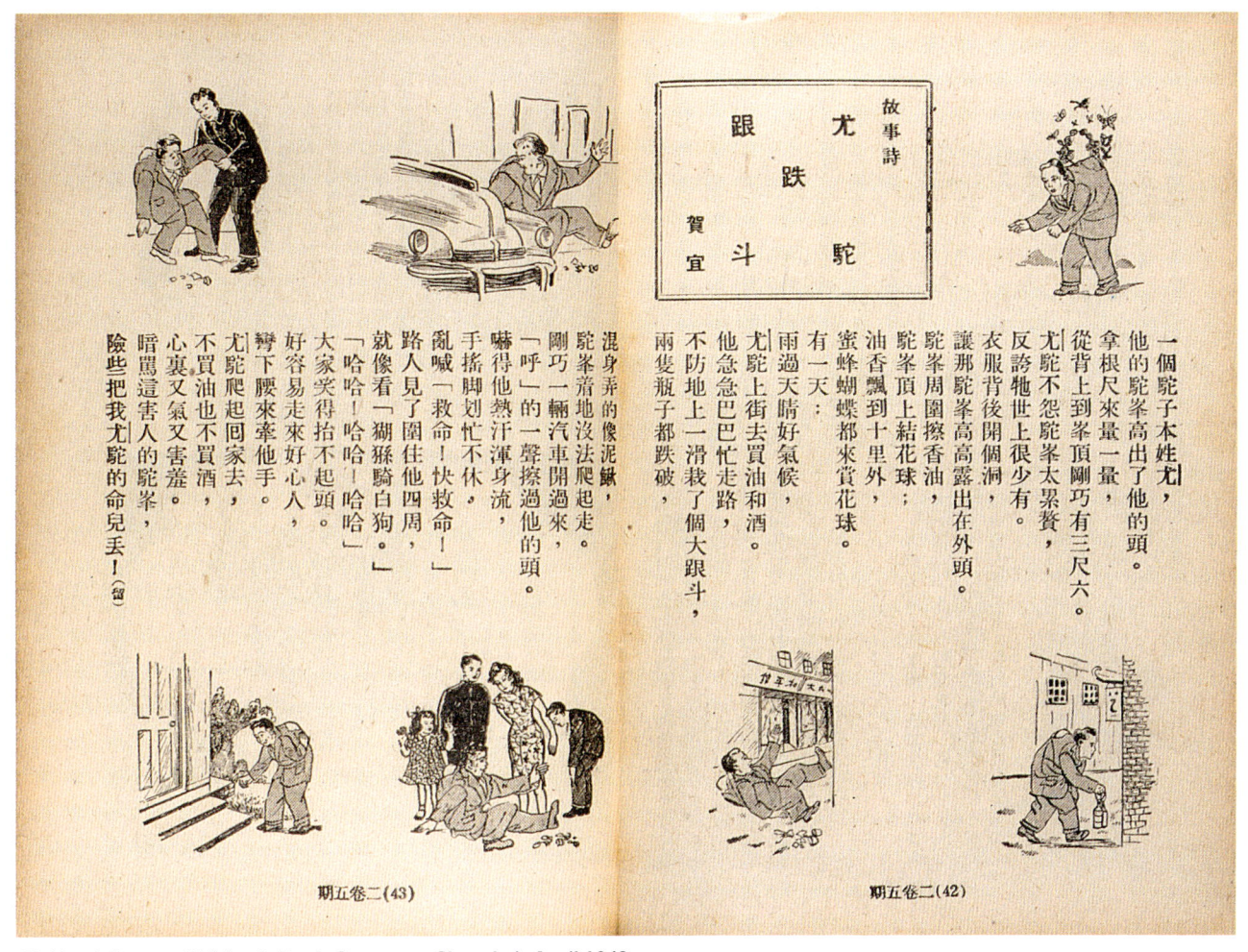

Children's Stories. **Children's Book Company, Shanghai, April 1948.**

Camelback You Turns a Somersault (You is a Chinese surname)

There once was a hunchback called You,
Whose hump over his head proudly rose.
When measured with a stick, from his back to its peak,
It extended six inches and three feet.

Camelback You never once complained,
That his hunchback caused him endless pain.
On the contrary he boasted, his nose in the air,
That his brilliant hunchback was without compare.

There's a hole cut in the back of his clothes,
Where the hunchback sticks out and is grandly exposed.

All around his fine hunchback he rubs fragrant oil,
And at the top of the hunchback are flowers in a coil.

The perfume can be smelled from as far as ten miles,
Bees and butterflies are seduced by its wiles.

One day after raining the weather turned fine,
So You went out shopping for oil and wine.

He was walking so fast, it wasn't his fault,
That he tripped and turned a quick somersault.

The two empty bottles dropped down and were smashed,
Like his entire body with mud was splashed.

At that very moment as he lay on the ground,
A car drove by, he was scared by the sound.
"Honk" went the horn and it should be said,
As the car drove by You got bumped in the head.
He was so overwrought that his sweat began to flow,
With arms and legs flailing, he made quite a show.

He shouted aloud "Help me, I say!"
The people in the street, as there was no reason to pay,
Formed a circle around him, to enjoy the cruel play.
You don't see a monkey riding on a dog's back every day!

The crowd found this so funny, they quite split their sides,
Until one came to help him, a man who was kind.

He approached poor Camelback and extended his hand,
He helped Camelback rise but he barely could stand.

He never bought oil, he never bought wine,
He went home angry and ashamed for the very first time.

He secretly cursed his trouble-making hump,
"You almost finished me off, you son of a gun."

1940s

Chinese Brush Painting, for Primary and Middle Schools, 4 volumes. Wanye Book Company, Shanghai, 1946.
Feng Zikai (1898–1975), one of the most important Chinese scholar-painters of the 20th century, comes as close as any Chinese of his period to being a "renaissance man." His stories, cartoons and illustrations for children appear in many important Chinese children's magazines from the 1930s to the 1970s. A Buddhist who had studied in Japan and who was equally conversant in Chinese and Western literature, and wrote books about Western music and Buddhist philosophy, Feng was victimized in the Cultural Revolution, and died in 1975.

A Close Resemblance

The Moon is Waiting For Us

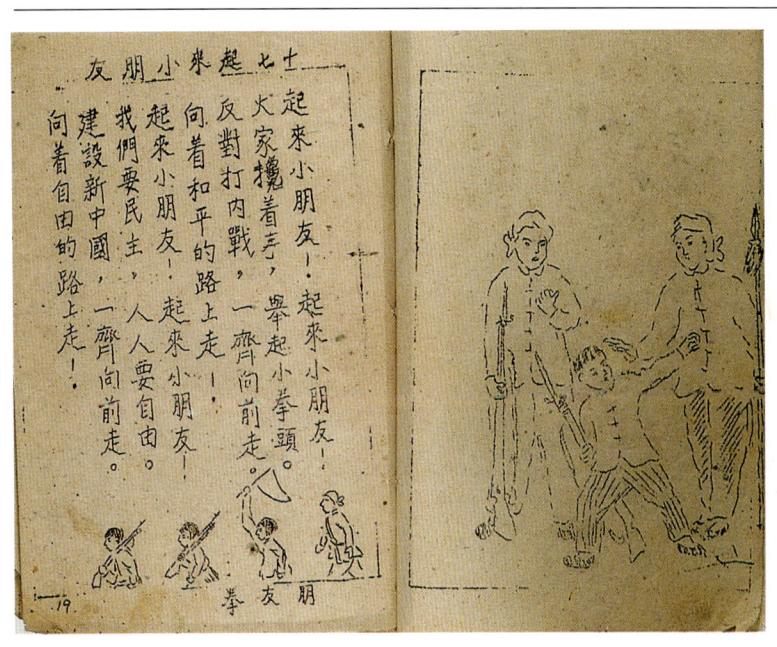

Chinese Language Textbook for Lower Primary School, Volume 3. Edited by the education department of the Border Region Administrative Committee of the Jin/Cha/Ji Border Region. No date, ca. 1946–47.
After establishing a base in Yanan, northern Shaanxi, in 1937, the Chinese Communist Party, with the cooperation of the nationalists, established two border region governments, one of which is the Jin/Cha/Ji area, comprising parts of Shanxi, Chahar and Hebei. The border areas edited their own textbooks and had them printed in different locations in the districts. Border region books are printed by xylography, woodblock or movable type on rough paper and bound in the simplest fashion.

Chapter 17: Rise Up, Young Friends

Rise up young friends! Rise up young friends!
Everyone raise your hands, and make fists in the air.
Opposing the civil war, together we march forward.
Moving in the direction of peace.

Rise up young friends! Rise up young friends!
We want democracy, so everyone can be free.
Let us build a New China, together we march forward.

Combined Chinese Language and Useful Knowledge Textbook, for Lower Primary Schools, Volume 8. Daiyue, Shanxi, Xinhua Bookstore, September, 1947.

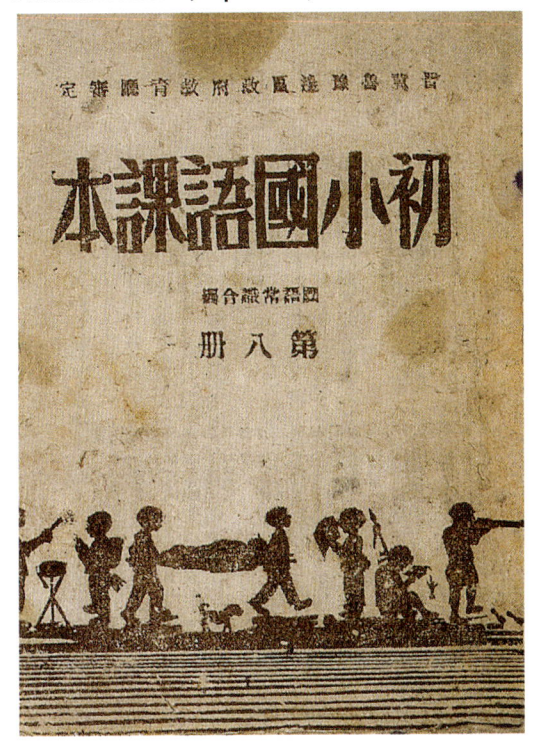

Like the Jin/Cha/Ji regional government, the Jin/Ji/Lu/Yu (Shanxi, Hebei, Shandong, Henan) border area edited its own textbooks. The cover shows silhouettes of boy soldiers in wartime.

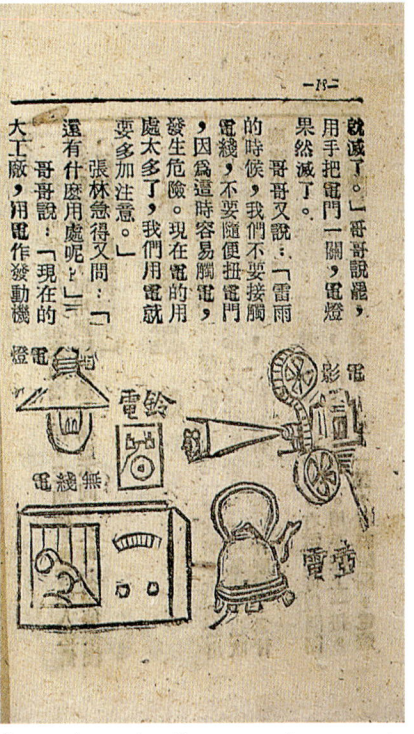

This rough woodcut illustrates a chapter on the uses of electricity.

New Children's World magazine. New Children's World Press (Commercial Press), Shanghai, September 15, 1949.
The cover of this Commercial Press magazine, published weeks before the establishment of the People's Republic of China on October 1, shows children, some in patched clothing, pinning stars on the uniforms of soldiers of the People's Liberation Army and presenting them with daily necessities such as toothbrushes. Here the soldiers in their cotton shoes and puttees are presented as casual, approachable and hardly intimidating, a far cry from the heroic aspect they would take on a decade later.

The Seventeen Good Years 1949–66

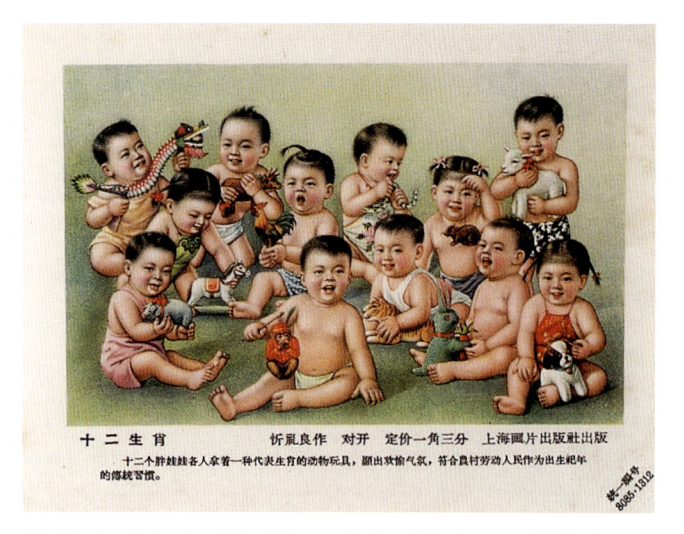

The Twelve Animals of the Chinese Zodiac. No date, ca. 1956.
A reduced version of a wall poster. The twelve signs of the Chinese zodiac are represented by animals. In China, one belongs to a certain sign depending on the year of one's birth, rather than the month, as in the Western zodiac. The 12 Chinese "year" animals are dragon, snake, bull, horse, pig, dog, rat, rabbit, tiger, sheep, monkey, cock. The caption explains that the animals were used by "working people in the countryside" to remember the year of their birth.

China Youth and Children magazine. Beijing, April 28, 1951.
The cover illustration, showing a factory worker's family with two children.

Kindergarten Object Recognition Pictures. Children's Reading Material Publishing Company, Shanghai, 1955.
A collection of 108 pictures of easily recognized objects, from animals, plants, clothing, vehicles and household objects to workers, peasants and soldiers. In the foreword, the suggestion is made to assign a different picture to each pre-literate child in lieu of their names.

New Children's World magazine. Shanghai, November 1, 1951.
Children dressed as a worker, peasant, soldier and urban intellectual take pot shots at a snooty capitalist, the American general Douglas MacArthur and G.I. Joe. The bandaged head of Chiang Kai-shek lies on the floor.

48

The Seventeen Good Years 1949–66

***Cutting and Pasting.* No publisher, no date. ca. 1950.**

The preface contains a discussion of the importance in China of "education in production." While admitting that it is impossible to turn the sort of cut-and-paste projects contained in the book into commercially saleable products, *"the practice of cutting and pasting can nurture in the child the kind of skills necessary for engaging in commercial production....The book has two purposes: to develop children's inherent intelligence; and to nourish in children the habit of, and interest in, productive work."*

Working

***Cut and Paste Workbook.* Andong, Chengwenxin Publishing Company, no date.**

Silhouette

***Gola and the Camels.* Youth and Children Press, Shanghai, 1956.**

A picture story set in Inner Mongolia. Gola and his parents live near a salt lake in the middle of the desert, where camels are the only means of transportation. Gola obtains his parents' permission to accompany a camel caravan delivering salt from the lake to the nearest railhead. After several days of travel, they nearly run out of water. Relying on the camels' natural instincts, they find a source of pure fresh water and refresh themselves there for a night. Three days later they arrive at the railhead. The adults' precis concludes with the following: "When railroads and highways extend to every corner of the country, we will no longer be frightened by the desert."

49

The Seventeen Good Years 1949–66

Primary School Chinese–Tibetan Bilingual Language Textbook. Cultural and Education Department, Qinghai Province People's Government, 1953.

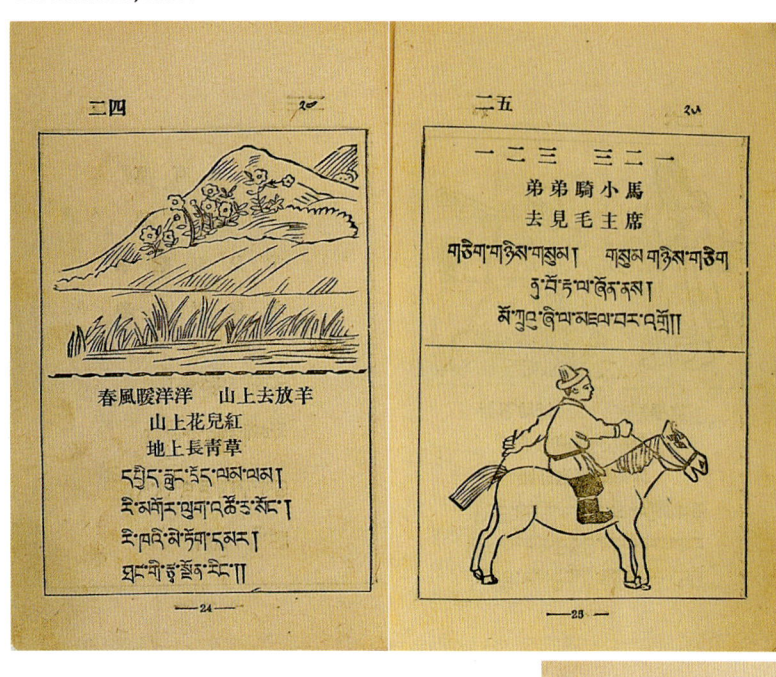

In 1950, the People's Liberation Army entered Tibet and Qinghai. The present volume was edited by the Department of Education of Qinghai province.

Left: *When the spring breezes blow, warm and gentle, we go up the mountain and let the sheep out to pasture. The flowers on the mountain are red, On the ground the tall grass is green.*

Right: *Little brother rides a pony And goes to see Chairman Mao.*

Left: *The People's Liberation Army loves the people. They have destroyed the man-eating wolves and tigers. They have saved the people from a living hell.*

Right: *Chairman Mao is brilliant and wise. He is the leader of the Communist Party. He is the leader of the People's Liberation Army. He has overseen the emancipation of the poor. He is the great liberator of the people.*

Hygiene Rhymes. Liaoning Art Publishing Company, Shenyang, 1959.

In addition to engaging in class struggle, children were encouraged to rid the country of various natural pests.

Left: *You clap "four" I clap "four" Kill the flies and the mosquitos.*

Right: *You clap "five" I clap "five" Destroy the rats and the sparrows.*

The Seventeen Good Years 1949–66

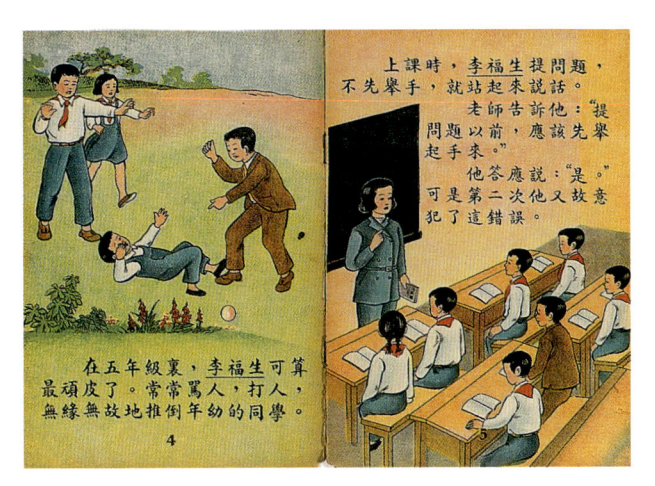

***The Red Kerchief*. Xiao pengyou Magazine Press, Shanghai, 1952.**
The red kerchief refers to the distinguishing kerchief of the Young Pioneers.

Left: *Li Fusheng was the naughtiest student in the fifth grade. He frequently used foul language, hit his classmates and for no reason often pushed pupils younger than himself down onto the ground.*

Right: *In class, Li Fusheng often stood up and asked questions without first raising his hand. The teacher told him: "You should raise your hand before you ask questions in class." He replied, "I will." But the next time he asked a question, he purposely made the same mistake.*

***Xiao Ying Cuts and Pastes*. Children's Reading Material Publishing Company, Shanghai, 1954.**
A picture story for nursery school children in which Xiao Ying's parents teach her to cooperate with her friends to obtain better results with her cutting and pasting project. The story is printed on the back cover of the book for teachers or parents to read.

***We Love Labor*. Youth and Children Publishing Company, Shanghai, 1961.**

A basketful of vegetables. Designed by Ding Shen.

***A Lazy Girl's Wish*. Foreign Language Press, Beijing, 1965.**
In this English translation, a lazy girl gets what she asks for—that everything should work on its own, without her having to lift a finger. But she soon pays a price for this. After being overwhelmed by such phenomena as huge quantities of food flying into her mouth on its own volition, she learns to take responsibility for herself.

The Seventeen Good Years 1949–66

Ah! How Beautiful is Our Factory! **Language Reform Publishing Company, Beijing, 1959.**
A kindergarten reader in *pinyin* romanization and Chinese characters teaching children how to get along with their schoolmates, and "educating them in the principles of collectivism." Children use shaming techniques to restore equilibrium.

She picked up a block, walked over to the table and said to Xiao Mao: "Xiao Mao, let's play together with the blocks."
Xiao Mao pouted but remained silent. When Rongrong realized that Xiao Mao was upset, she said loudly, "Mingming, Mingming, bring the blocks over here. Xiao Mao is really upset."

***I Want to Wear a Red Kerchief Too.* China Youth and Children Press, Beijing, 1958.**
A primary 2 reader extolling the virtues of the Young Pioneers organization.
Young Pioneers wore a distinctive red kerchief.

Left: Big sister wakes up early,
As soon as she gets up she sweeps the floor,
After she finishes sweeping, she does her morning exercises,
The sun shines and smiles upon both of us.

Right: Be attentive in class,
Concentrate on your homework,
Get full marks in every subject,
Memorize everything teacher says.

The Seventeen Good Years 1949–66

Illustrated Classroom Rules and Regulations for Middle School Students. Shanghai People's Art Publishing Company, 1956.
A set of school rules borrowed from the Soviet Union.

（六）上課時要坐端正，專心聽講，不隨便說話，不做其他事情。出入教室要得到教師的允許。

（七）回答教師提問時要起立，得到教師允許後再坐下。向教師發問時先舉手。

Left: *During class, sit up straight, concentrate on what is being said, do not speak out of turn, do nothing but school work. Obtain the teacher's permission before entering or leaving the classroom.*

Right: *When the teacher asks you a question, stand up when replying. Do not sit down before obtaining the teacher's permission. When asking the teacher a question, first raise your hand.*

Chairman Mao's Photograph. Children's Reading Material Publishing Company, 1955.

家裏沒有吃的，秋收之後，誰到地裏去撿散落的稻頭啊？地主家的大牯牛，大山羊，誰去餵，誰去放，誰去割乾草啊？天冷了，家家像冰窖一樣，要烤火，誰去上山打柴啊？爹娘給地主折磨得夠了，這不都是孩子的事嗎！

可是解放軍一來，毛主席的金光一照，他們也就跟着爹娘大伙兒，改樣兒過解放日子啦！

Left: *There was nothing to eat at home. After the autumn harvest, who will bother to go into the rice paddies and gather the scattered leftover rice? Who will feed the landlord's big bulls and goats and who will put them out to pasture? Who will cut the straw? When it gets so cold that everyone's house is as uncomfortable as an icehouse, who will go up into the hills and collect firewood? Now that Mother and Father are completely exhausted from working for the landlord, isn't it the children's responsibility to perform these tasks?*

Right: *But when the People's Liberation Army came to the village, and the golden light of Chairman Mao shone down upon us, the children, just like their Mother and Father, all enjoyed the fruits of liberation!*

The Seventeen Good Years 1949–66

Beautiful Colors. Dadong Publishing Company, Shanghai, 1950.
A simple picture book produced one year after the founding of the People's Republic.

Right: *Red, red, red. The sun in the east is red.*
Left: *Red, red, red. China has given birth to Mao Zedong.*

***Xiao pengyou* magazine. Shanghai, February 20, 1954.**
The revolutionary family of the early 1950s had three to five children, the more children, the more revolutionary the family. In this picture, there are three, but from Mother's rounded belly, perhaps revolutionary number four is on the way?

Father, Older Brother and I glance with gratitude at the picture of Chairman Mao hanging on the wall.

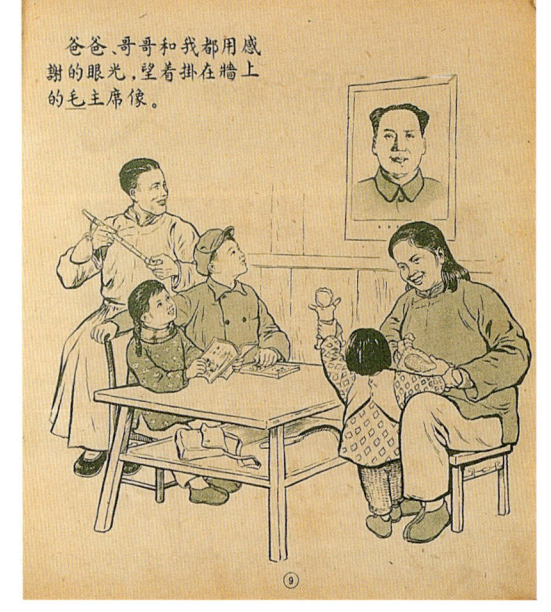

***Xiao pengyou* magazine. Shanghai, February 15, 1952.**

Left: *Painting portraits of the most lovable people*

Ah Xin loves to paint pictures,
He paints pictures of the most adorable people.
He paints Chairman Mao,
He paints Uncle Stalin.
When he finishes painting, he says:
"I donate these pictures to the Chinese volunteer soldiers in the hope that they will fight even harder against the vicious American 'wolves.'"

Right: "Look! See how the two Soviet children are playing with their blocks. They want to be engineers when they grow up. Come along! Let us learn from them and build our beloved Motherland."

The Seventeen Good Years 1949–66

The Sun Climbs Into the Window. Youth and Children Publishing Company, Shanghai, 1960.

Voluntary Labor Day. Youth and Children Publishing Company, Shanghai, 1963.
The first edition of this book was published in 1958, during the last years of Sino–Soviet friendship. The relationship came to an abrupt end in 1960, but by 1963, this book was reprinted, and the friendly, approachable portrait of Lenin mingling with the masses on Labor Day, by the Chinese artist Hua Sanchuan, is a reminder that China retained an ideological attachment to Lenin and Leninism.

I Came By Train. Children's Reading Material Press, Shanghai, 1955.
In this attractive picture story, an old man who never had the luxury of riding in a bullock cart gets to take a short ride on a new train. In the caption, the old man thinks to himself: *Well, an old man like me finally gets to ride on a train! If liberation [1949] came a few years later than it did, I would have been worked to death by the landlord, or I would have simply died of old age! Who could ever imagine that an old man like me who never rode on a bullock cart actually took a ride on a train! I owe all my good fortune to Chairman Mao...*

Xiao pengyou magazine. Shanghai, April 20, 1950.
Before the adaption of *pinyin* as the official system of romanization, China experimented with several different forms of transcribing the Chinese language into the Western alphabet, hence the name of the magazine written as SIAO PUNGJU. In *pinyin* it is rendered *Xiao pengyou*.

The Seventeen Good Years 1949–66

Xiao pengyou magazine. Shanghai, April 25, 1952.
The signs the children are holding repeat the contents of the text translated below, but in addition one girl carries a sign that reads "Wear cotton shoes," presumably rather than more extravagant leather shoes.

A Train Called "Thrifty"

Woo, Woo, Woo
The train called "Thrifty" blows its whistle.
To all the thrifty children, it says:

Don't waste pens and erasers,
Don't invite friends to parties on your birthday,
Don't buy too many toys,
Don't waste water,
Don't waste electricity.

Car by car,
The train called "Thrifty" gets longer and longer,
Carrying its message swiftly,
To every corner of China.

Left: *Everyone is learning how to sing.*

Everyone is doing their tasks.

Only this one is lazy. Look how comfortable he is, Sleeping on a branch!

Right: *Everyone has something to eat.*

The fruit is so sweet and delicious!

But little lazybones is crying, because he doesn't have anything to eat.

Why is he crying?

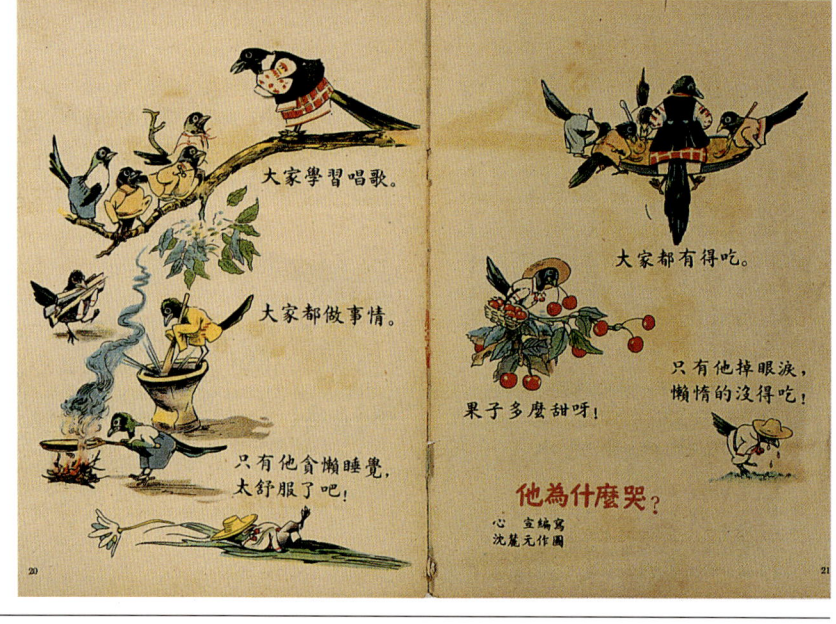

Winter Holiday Homework Book, Grade 4. Northeast Pictorial Press, Shanghai, 1954.
The cover picture shows a group of children presenting a rosette and a plaque to the mother of a solider who presumably perished during the Korean War. The plaque reads "Glorious Soldier's Family."

The Seventeen Good Years 1949–66

***Selected Pictures by Children.* Kaiming Bookstore, Beijing, 1950.**
Paintings by children living in northeastern China reflecting life in the 1940s, including examples of suffering during the Japanese occupation.

Collecting water from a well.

During the winter, the Japanese devils confiscated our cotton-lined clothing, explaining that they would make cotton clothing for us with it. Needless to say, they never brought us any cotton clothing, and we froze through the winter.

***The Volunteer Soldiers Love Korean Children.* Xiao pengyou Publishing Company, Shanghai, 1952.**

After the enemy planes flew away, they [the soldiers] helped the children find their mother. After searching a while, they finally found her. The children shouted: "The Chinese People's Volunteer Soldiers are great! The Chinese People's Volunteer Soldiers are great!"

***Attacking Bandit Chiang.* Dadong Publishing Company, Shanghai, June, 1950.**
In this baldly propagandistic assault on Chiang Kai-shek, published in 1950, children make a snowman that resembles Chiang Kai-shek, and proceed to destroy it. The library's copy is an uncut publisher's proof copy, raising the question of whether the book was ever formally published.

Right: *Bandit Chiang is an evil person. Just looking at him is enough to make you hate him.*

Left: *Such a close resemblance! When the black dog saw the snowman, it began to bark. Then the dog leaped and bit off Bandit Chiang's mouth.*

57

The Seventeen Good Years 1949–66

I Love People from the Soviet Union. New Art Publishing Company, Shanghai, 1953.

From the preface: *The great friendship between the peoples of the Soviet Union and China is indescribable! The U.S.S.R. helped China to defeat the Japanese devils, aided us in economic construction, sent numerous specialists to assist us in the work of national construction and shared with us their advanced experience. When one thinks of the unassailable friendship between the peoples of the Soviet Union and China, a single thought comes to mind: "I Love People from the Soviet Union!"*

From the bottom of their hearts, the villagers shouted: "Long live Stalin!"

***Riding to Beijing on Horseback.* Children's Reading Material Publishing Company, Shanghai, 1955.**
A song book including such numbers as "The Ballad of the Wheat Harvest," "Kicking the Shuttlecock," "Making a Visit of Conciliation to a People's Liberation Army Family," "Sino-Soviet Friendship is Good," "It is a Way of Ensuring Peace," and "Let's All Get Vaccinated with BCG Vaccine." On the cover, children dressed as workers, peasants and soldiers salute two mounted friends as they ride to the capital.

The Seventeen Good Years 1949–66

Xiao pengyou magazine. Shanghai, November 5, 1954.
"Visiting the Soviet Exhibition Hall." Now called the Beijing Exhibition Hall, this fine example of Soviet wedding-cake architecture, built as a gift of Sino–Soviet friendship during the first four years of the People's Republic, stands next to the Beijing Zoo.

Xiao pengyou magazine. Shanghai, November 5, 1954.
"Picking Fruit," painted by Chen Xianqi, layout by Chen Xiongxiu.

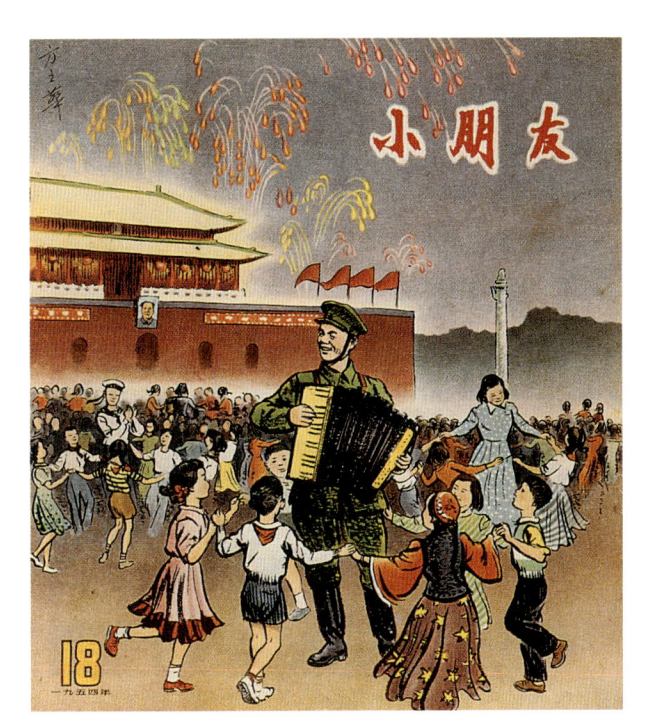

Xiao pengyou magazine. Shanghai, September 20, 1954.
"In the Evening on National Day." Tiananmen Square in Beijing has long been the site of China's National Day celebrations on October 1. The leadership would make a public appearance atop Chairman Mao's portrait on the rostrum on Tiananmen Gate, the large structure illustrated here. Joining the soldier's circle in the illustration is a girl in Uighur dress.

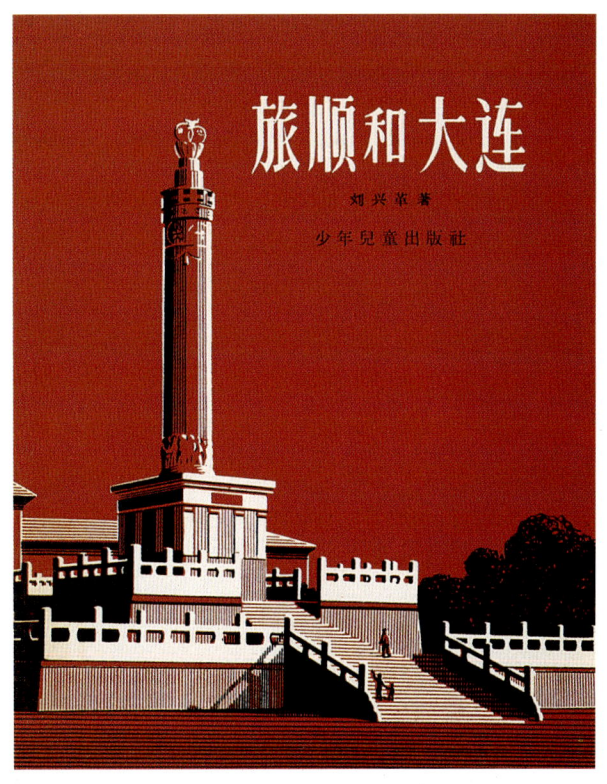

Lüshun and Dalian. Youth and Children Publishing Company, Shanghai, 1957.
The history and features of the twin port cities of Lüshun and Dalian, together called Lüda, which lie at the southern tip of the Liaodong peninsula in northeast China. The book cover shows the rather stark Monument to Sino–Soviet Friendship in Lüshun.

The Seventeen Good Years 1949–66

Beautiful Shanghai. Youth and Children Publishing Company, Shanghai, 1962.
Fine propaganda for China's greatest city. Accompanying a picture of a park is the following caption: *In the park near the Bund, older people are performing calsthenics, children are singing and playing. Before Liberation, the imperialists had a wooden sign hanging at the entrance to the park. It read "No Chinese or dogs allowed." The imperialists prevented Chinese people from enjoying themselves on their very own territory.*
However, around 1996, a mainland Chinese newspaper admitted that the inscription on the sign had been fabricated for propaganda purposes in the 1950s. On the actual sign in question, one line read "No dogs allowed," while a separate line read "No Chinese domestic helpers allowed entry without their charges."

The old Temple of the City God district and the Bridge of Nine Bends are always bustling with great crowds, as if a temple fair took place there every day. From an endless number of stands, all sorts of wonderful things are sold. Nearby is Yu Garden, with its exquisite pavilions and beautiful towers. It was here that the heroes of the Small Sword Society [1853–54] organized their anti-imperialist activities.

Beautiful Shanghai! The number one industrial city in the Motherland, the birthplace of the Chinese Commnist Party. Oh Shanghai, we salute you, we sing your praises!

Guerrilla Fighters in the African Jungle. Youth and Children Publishing Company, Shanghai, 1959.
From the 1950s to the 1980s, China saw herself as a champion of the Third World, and provided aid to many countries in Africa as a way of enticing them away from Western influence.

From the preface: *Cameroon is a country on the African continent. It is very hot there, and the land is covered with dense jungle. Cameroon is rich in natural resources. However, this fine country has been invaded and occupied by imperialists for the past several hundred years. In 1916, English and French imperialists occupied Cameroon, and cruelly oppressed the Cameroon people.*

To attain freedom and independence for their motherland, the strong and daring Cameroon people have fought a continuing battle against the imperialists. They organized guerrilla armies to strike fiercely at the aggressors. We firmly believe that the courageous Cameroon people will attain the ultimate victory.

Some soldiers of the French invading army were killed, others were taken prisoner. The old man even took up a rifle, and managed to capture two French soldiers alive. He was a guerrilla fighter too!

The Seventeen Good Years 1949–66

Children of the Sun. Youth and Children Publishing Company, Shanghai, 1961.
A strange tale in picture story form centered on the space race and Sino–Soviet friendship, with America ending up in disgrace.

The sun and stars warmly greet their first visitor from afar, a Soviet rocket.

The happy Soviet rocket before takeoff.

The American rocket fizzles.

The sun introduces the rocket to his nine sons, the stars, and they quickly grow so close that the sun regards the rockets as his tenth son. When the moon rises, the stars ask her to tell them a bedtime story.

She begins: "There are two different kinds of places in the world. In the first kind of place, people are happy: they work, they sing, and they don't lack food and clothing…"

The Soviet rocket says, "My home is just like that. And there is another happy place like that. It's called China."

The Moon says: "Yes, you are right. But in the second kind of place, life is quite different. In that kind of place, everything is run by a small number of big bosses, all of them big and fat. The millions of other people who live there are hungry all the time…."

As they watch "that" place, a strange black object standing on the ground starts to shake and rises slowly into the air. One of the fat men announces: "We are also sending a man into outer space to be a guest there. He has already taken off. And in only one minute…." But before he finishes the sentence, the black object turns a somersault in the air and falls, "kaplop," into a lake.

The stars ask: "Why did that man change his mind and turn back? Why doesn't he want to come here and be our guest too?"

The next day, the moon told the sun what had taken place the night before. The sun said, "That is indeed strange. They said they were going to send someone here to be our guest. I wonder why he isn't here now."

At this moment, a news report arrived, delivered by the wind. It read: "The man the United States was attempting to send to the sun's house crashed on takeoff!"

The Seventeen Good Years 1949–66

Song of the Swallows. Music Publishing Company, Beijing, 1958.

Two children holding a hammer and sickle ride a rocket into the future—a youthful symbol of the Great Leap Forward. The Great Leap Forward (1957–59) was a campaign launched by Mao to lift China out of economic backwardness by mobilizing the masses to produce "more, faster, better, and more cheaply." Results, however, fell far short of expectations.

The Young Expert. Liaoning People's Publishing Company, Shenyang, 1958.

A collection of rhymes for children from the Great Leap Forward period. Topics include descriptions of children destroying the "four pests" (mosquitos, flies, rats, sparrows), collecting nightsoil and repairing irrigation systems. The cover shows a boy who is an accomplished poacher of sparrows. When it became apparent that sparrows were actually instrumental in limiting pests, they were replaced by bedbugs as a target for extermination.

The Seventeen Good Years 1949–66

***Premier Zhou Enlai Visits the Children's Palace.* Youth and Children Publishing Company, Shanghai, 1961.**
Members of the Young Pioneers organization carried out various extracurricular activities at Children's Palaces throughout China.

In the airplane model class, there is a model of a passenger jet. Premier Zhou says: "This is a well made airplane. I hope you make some more new models, like a space rocket. Then you can travel from planet to planet."

***The Secret of the Walnuts.* Changjiang Literature and Art Publishing Company, Wuhan, 1959.**
The title story in this anthology is a sentimental tale about a young girl who flees her home in Shandong alone and makes her way to the communist base at Yanan. She steals a single unripe walnut from a tree belonging to a local woman, whose kindness and generosity teaches her a lesson.

***A Basket.* Ningxia People's Publishing Company, Yinchuan, 1963.**
A simple tale in which a boy returns a book a solider loses, and a kindly older woman the shopping basket the boy loses. In the end, the boy's mother says to her son, "You are Chairman Mao's child."

The Seventeen Good Years 1949–66

Youth and Children's Drawing and Painting, Fourth Grade. Youth and Children Publishing Company, Shanghai, 1963.

Cover illustration showing the farmer as a children's hero.

Picture for tracing and copying entitled "Reading New Books."

What Do We Learn in Kingergarten? Shanghai Education Publishing Company, 1959.
Pedagogical guidelines for kindergarten teachers.

Observing adults at work

From the preface: *According to local conditions, kindergarten teachers can arrange for children to watch adults working at tasks that the children can understand. In the countryside, for example, they can watch commune members working in the fields: planting seeds in the spring, harvesting crops in the fall, digging canals, collecting nightsoil for fertilizer, etc. By observing this kind of work, children will learn that a happy life is the result of hard work performed by their mothers, fathers, aunts and uncles, under the leadership of the Communist Party. In this way they will come to appreciate the importance of labor, to love labor and the working people, and to cherish the results of labor.*

The Seventeen Good Years 1949–66

A selection of children's songbooks from the 1960s.

The Seventeen Good Years 1949–66

The People's Communes are Really Good. Youth and Children Publishing Company, Shanghai, 1959.

An introduction to the virtues of the commune system.

When the whistle blows,
Everyone to the canteen goes;
The food there is as delicious as can be,
And best of all, it's always free.

Everyone Says the Communes Are Good. Youth and Children Publishing Company, Shanghai, 1960.

One goal of Mao Zedong's Great Leap Forward was to turn China into a utopian socialist paradise with a developed industrial base in the remarkably short period of five years. This illustration reflects the naïve expectations of materialistic comfort. By 1963, some 35 million Chinese farmers (the figure published by the Chinese government; the number may be as high as 45 million), many of them living in such communes, had starved to death. The Soviet Union had disapproved of the formation of the communes, one factor in the 1960 Sino–Soviet split.

Everyone in the Commune Moves into a New Home
By Xu Qingshan

One person smiles,
Everyone smiles.
One family smiles,
Every family smiles.
Happiness spreads to every corner of the commune,
Everyone in the commune moves into a new home.

The Struggle of the People of Taiwan. Youth and Children Publishing Company, Shanghai, 1958.

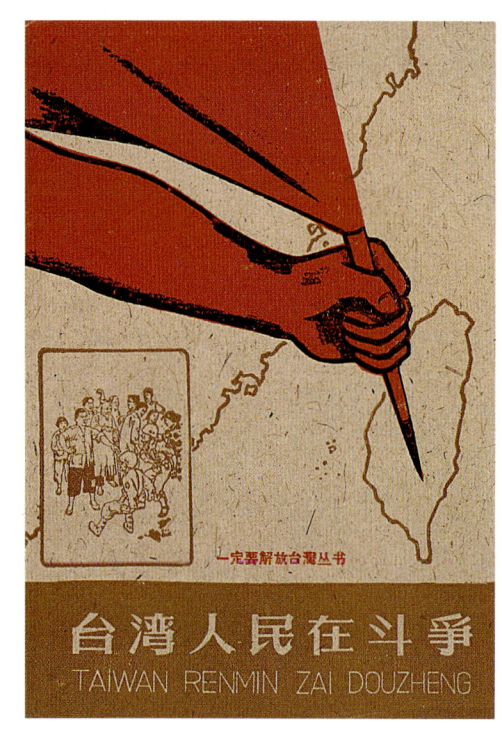

Taiwan is an inseparable part of China. We cannot stand aside and allow nine million of our compatriots to suffer as they do at present. Regardless of how shamelessly the American imperialists behave, we will definitely liberate Taiwan, and toss both the American imperialists and Chiang Kai-shek into the sea.

The Seventeen Good Years 1949–66

Love Labour. No date.
Packing label for export product.

***Xiao pengyou* magazine. Shanghai, October 11, 1958.**
Children played an active role in collecting scrap metal for the backyard furnaces that played an important role in the Great Leap Forward.

Come everybody, let's fight the drought and help out in the drive for industrialization.

We Love Labor. China Youth and Children Publishing Company, Beijing, 1959.

Left: *There is an empty lot next to the building. We go there to collect the broken bricks and roof tiles. We also dig little holes there, and plant the castor-oil plant and sunflowers.*

Right: *There is also an empty lot next to the trellis. Here we pick the weeds, turn the soil, dig holes, collect broken bricks and roof tiles, and plant the castor-oil plant and sunflowers.*

The Seventeen Good Years 1949–66

Trapping Sparrows. **China Record Company, Shanghai, no date, ca. 1955.**

A floppy 78 rpm record to provide background music to the campaign to wipe out the four pests: flies, mosquitos, rats and sparrows. The song is performed by the Children's Broadcast Choir of the Shanghai People's Radio Station. Abstract of the lyrics:

A flock of sparrows peeping and cheeping,
Flying around looking for something to eat.
When the Young Pioneers appear on the scene,
The little birds are frightened out of their wits.
We will catch them, pursue them, and wipe them out once and for all.
No longer will the grain of the Motherland go to waste.

Cover of a student notebook. Picture is titled and dated, "Destroy the Four Pests, January 1956."

With slingshot and spray gun, two children attempt to eradicate flies, mosquitos, rats and sparrows, all presented anthropomorphically. The trapped rat with bandaged paw is about to nibble on a family grain-register book. (Grain was subsidized in China up to the early 1980s.) The sparrows are wearing clothing that might associate them with the bourgeois class.

1. ***I Love Iron, I Love Steel.*** **China Youth and Children Publishing Company, Beijing, 1959.**
   A supplementary reader for first grade students, rich in Great Leap Forward ideology. Mao's campaign to overtake Britain's industrial output by 1974 involved a mass movement in which people attempted to refine iron and steel in primitive "backyard" blast furnaces. This cartoon-like illustration captures the arrogance of the time. The waste of resources producing poor quality metal was one factor in the devastating famine of the early 1960s.

   Come on everybody! Let's make iron.
   Come on everybody! Let's make steel.
   In less than 15 years,
   We will catch up with Great Britain.

2. ***Little Companion's Songbook.*** **Shanghai Literature and Art Publishing Company, 1958.**
   The cover shows children dancing around a cauldron of molten steel.

The Seventeen Good Years 1949–66

***Kindergarten Arts and Crafts Workbook, Upper Kindergarten.* Heyi Stationery Company, Jiangbei, Yongjia County, Zhejiang, no date.**
In the 1950s, adults from humble backgrounds would lecture students about how they suffered before the Communist revolution in 1949, and how life had improved subsequently. This practice was called *yi ku si tian*, the four characters to the left of this picture, literally, "Recall bitterness and contemplate sweetness." In this exercise, the student cuts out the characters and pastes them in the spaces at the top of the picture, in the style of a propaganda poster.

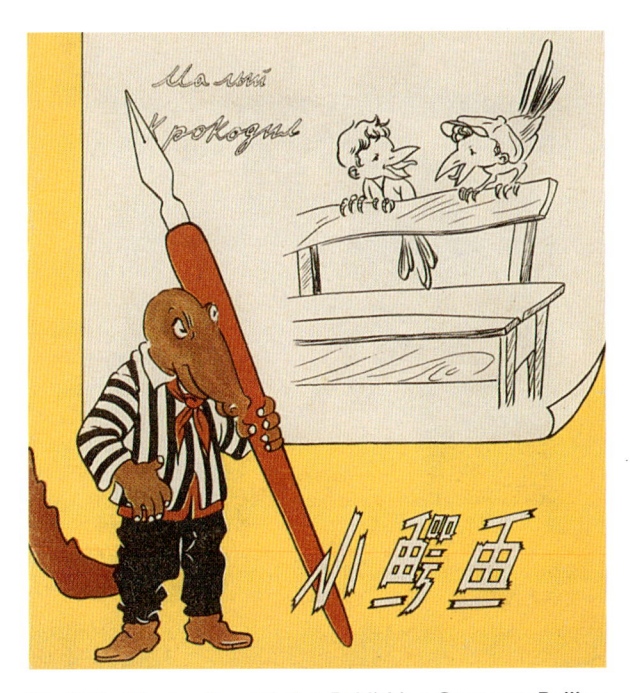

***The Little Alligator.* People's Art Publishing Company, Beijing, 1958.**
Translation of a Russian story of two Young Pioneers who start a "wall newspaper" entitled *The Little Alligator* in which they criticize the behavior of their fellow students. At first, the paper receives both praise and blame from the students, but before long, those who disapprove of it come to see that the paper's truthfulness in reporting is actually a virtue.

***Our Friends.* Youth and Children Publishing Company, Shanghai, 1959.**
A collection of Romanian stories for children that take the form of satires on children's bad study and living habits. The cover is by a Romanian artist.

The Seventeen Good Years 1949–66

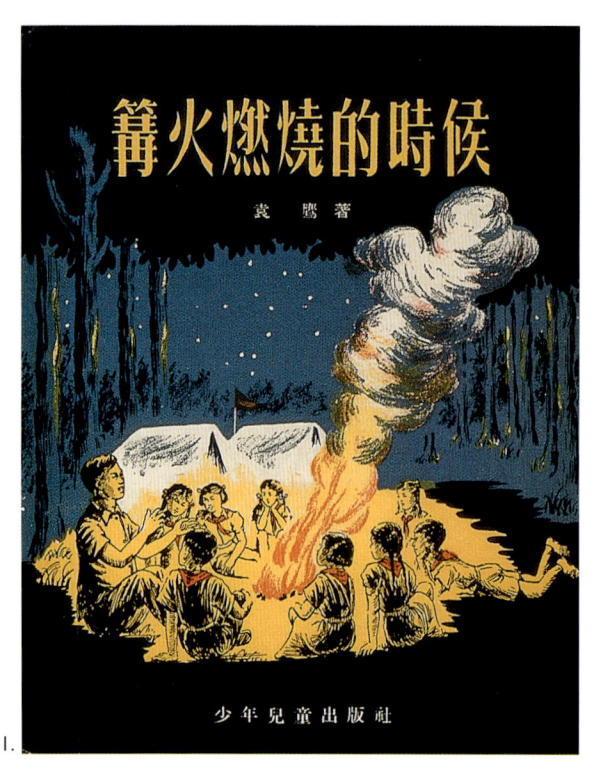

1. ***When the Bonfire Burned.*** **Youth and Children Publishing Company, Shanghai, 1955.**
   A poetry anthology. As described in the introduction, the prize-winning poem, "A Poem Sent to the Thames River," exposes how American imperialism cruelly injured the "peace soldiers" Julius and Ethel Rosenberg and tortured their children, while demonstrating how the people of China sympathize with and care deeply about the people who live in capitalist countries.

2. ***Tales of the Jungle.*** **Youth and Children Publishing Company, Shanghai, 1958.**
   A translation of Argentine author Horacio Quiroga's *Cuentos de la Selva* (1950), a collection of stories for children based on the author's experience of living in the jungle and his encounters with rare and extraordinary animals there.

3. ***The Naughty Bear.*** **Youth and Children Publishing Company, Shanghai, 1957.**
   Animal stories from the Soviet Union.

4. ***The Tale of Mt. Mushtak.*** **Youth and Children Publishing Company, Shanghai, 1957.**
   In this Uighur tale set in a village at the foot of Mt. Mushtak, a beautiful maiden falls in love with a boy, but her mother refuses to let her marry him because he is poor. As an ultimate test, the girl's mother tells the boy that if he is able to pluck a magic flower from the peak of Mt. Mushtak, she will allow the two of them to marry. Risking his life for love, the boy climbs to the top of the mountain, picks a flower, and eventually marries the girl.

The Seventeen Good Years 1949–66

Shadow Play. *Children's Reading Material Publishing Company, Shanghai,* 1955.
A how-to book for young children.

I want to make a dove of peace.

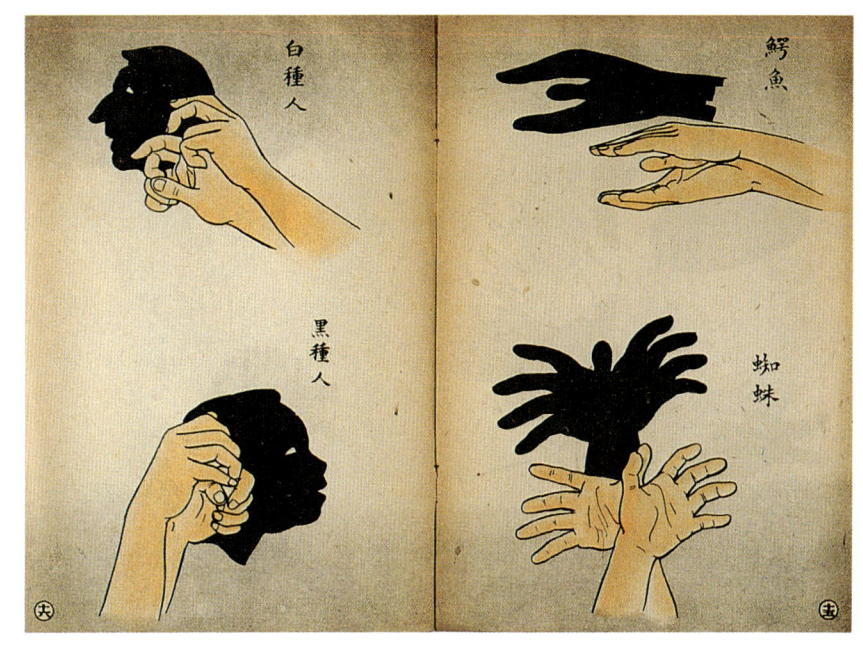

Upper left: *Caucasian man*
Lower left: *Negro man*
Upper right: *Alligator*
Lower right: *Spider*

Postcard. *I want to make a dove of peace.* By Fang Jing. Beijing, 1955.

Middle School Art Textbook, Volume 1. **Shanghai Primary and Middle School Textbook Compilation Group, 1977.**
The caption reads, "Unity, struggle, friendship." Representatives of the three major "races" portrayed with remarkable uniformity of age, expression and haircut.

The Seventeen Good Years 1949–66

The Little Negro Smiled. *Chung Hwa Book Company Shanghai, 1952.*
In this sentimental tale devoid of racial stereotypes, a Chinese girl succeeds in making an unfortunate "little Negro" doll happy.

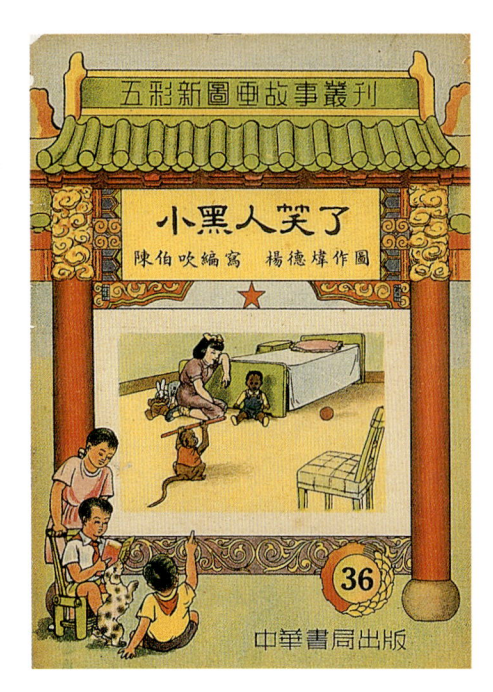

This little story book opens with a note to the reader: *Please read this first: The reactionary government of United States oppresses and tortures black people at every opportunity (and also oppresses and tortures the working people). We cannot tolerate this kind of imperialistic plot!*

In the story, a little girl buys a Negro boy doll made out of leather, but he always appears sad, no matter how hard she tries to make him feel happy. One night, her mother draws a few teeth on the boy's face with chalk, making it appear as if he is smiling. But Mother reminds her daughter that while the Negro doll may be happy, his parents in the United States are suffering at the hands of the American government.

Left: *The big white horse didn't move, but the little Negro was unable to stay upright on the horse, and fell onto the ground. Xiao Mei quickly picked him up, and when she looked at his face, she noticed that he was even more unhappy.*

Right: *It was getting dark outside. Xiaomei put a kerosene lamp near the little Negro. She thought that if he had some light, he might smile.*

In the United States, a Child was Murdered. *Youth and Children Publishing Company, Shanghai, 1958.*
An anthology of poems about children in the United States. The title poem is about an innocent black boy who is accused of having insulted a white woman shopkeeper by whistling at her. A lynch mob takes him from his home, kills him and tosses his body, trussed up in wire, into the Talahassee River. Another poem asks the question: What will American children grow up to be, if they only read comic books about crime, murder, corpses, the atomic bomb, a knife stuck into an infant's belly? According to the introduction, "The poems in this book condemn the evils of American society, but at the same time expresses the Chinese's people's concern for people who live in capitalist countries."

The Seventeen Good Years 1949–66

Chinese Language Textbook for Singapore and Malaysia. Chung Hwa Book Company, Hong Kong, 1957.

From a boat, presumably the Star Ferry, two children gaze at the Central district of Hong Kong island, 15 years before an economic miracle transformed this vista into a forest of skyscrapers.

I have a lot of good friends. Some of my friends are Malay, some of my friends are Indian, some are English. We all live close by each other, so we play together all the time. Sometimes we play ball, sometimes we go on little adventures. We all get along very well.

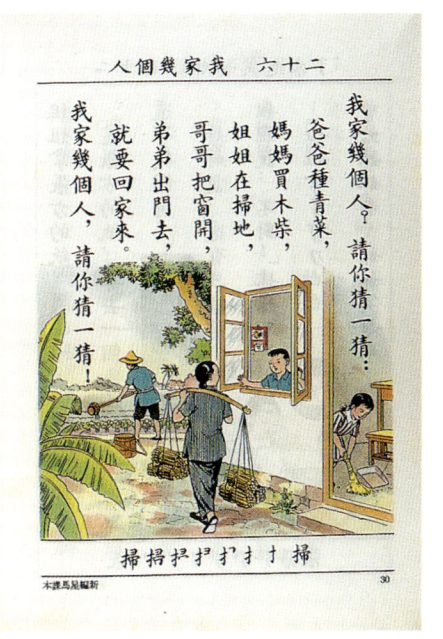

How many people are in my family? Please guess:
Daddy plants cabbage,
Mommy buys firewood,
Older Sister is sweeping the floor,
Older Brother is opening the window,
Little Brother went out,
But he will be home soon.
How many people are in my family?
Please guess!

Dai Language Primary School Arithmetic, Volume 1. Experimental edition. Xishuangbanna Autonomous Prefecture Textbook Compilation Office, Yunnan, 1956.
In the 1950s, textbooks in minority languages were introduced in Chinese schools. The practice ended during the Cultural Revolution. Minority textbooks were revived in the 1980s in some places, but rarely go beyond the primary or lower middle-school level.

This textbook is in the Xishuangbanna dialect of the Dai language, spoken in southern Yunnan. A separate edition was published in the Dai language dialect of northern Yunnan.

Children in Dai and Han Chinese dress gather in front of the entrance to their school. Below, embroidered Dai shoulder bags and the cover of the book are used in the illustrations to teach counting.

73

Cultural Revolution 1966–76

Revolutionary Cultural Activities and Physical Education, for Shanghai Kindergartens. Shanghai Municipal Primary and Middle School Textbook Compilation Group, Shanghai, 1972.

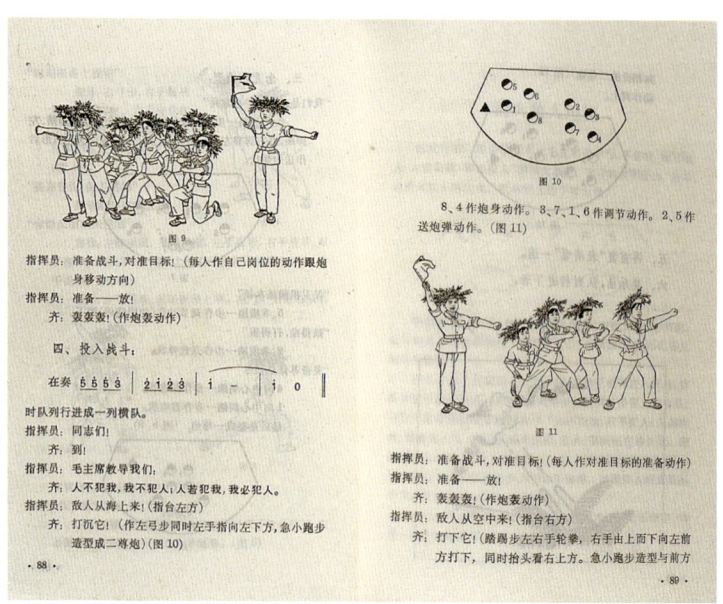

Script for a children's revolutionary dance drama, *We Are The Little Red Guards*.

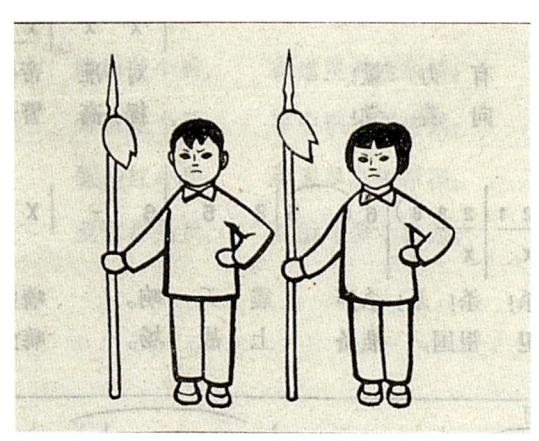

Be ready at any moment to attack the jackals and wolves.

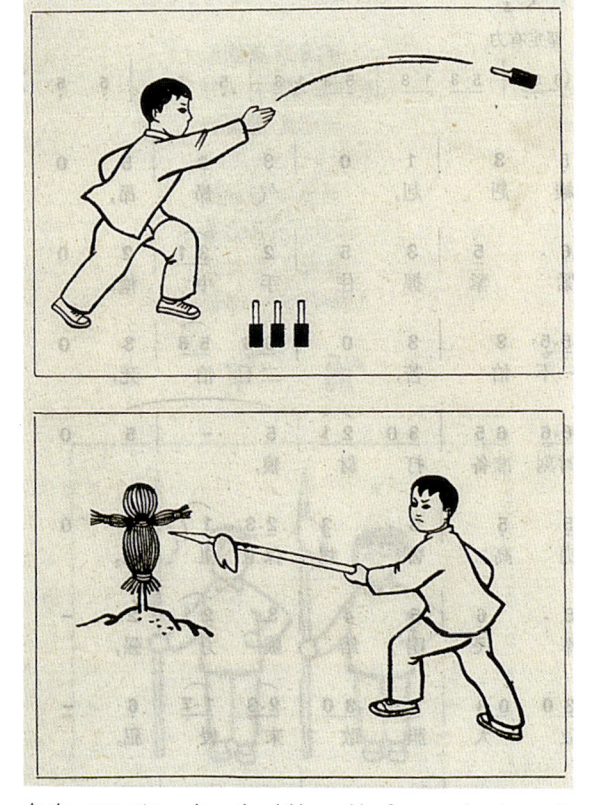

In the upper picture, have the children add a few more hand grenades to the picture. In the lower picture, have the children draw a red-tasseled spear.

Cultural Revolution 1966–76

***Arithmetic, for Fourth Grade Primary Schools in Shanghai.* Shanghai Primary and Middle School Textbook Compilation Group, 1970.**
The cover shows a rural classroom during the Cultural Revolution, with a peasant teacher. The teacher and students are holding up the "Little Red Book" of Chairman Mao's sayings. The inscription on the wall is Mao's calligraphic rendering of his famous injunction: "Study well. Make progress every day." The sunflowers on the wall recall the identification of students with sunflowers, always facing the sun—Chairman Mao.

***Walking Towards the Sun.* Youth and Children Press, Shanghai, 1966.**
A long narrative poem about the revolutionary activities of a South Vietnamese boy and his struggle against the Americans.

Cultural Revolution 1966–76

Xiao pengyou magazine. Shanghai, May 1966.
A panoramic satire on the American presence in Vietnam during the Vietnam War.

Cultural Revolution 1966–76

Little Red Guards Sing in Praise of the Red Satellite. Shanghai People's Publishing Company, 1970.
On April 24, 1970, China launched its first satellite, *Dong Fang Hong-1*. Its main purpose was propagandistic; the satellite performed few other functions but to broadcast the song, *The East is Red (Dong fang hong)*, a hymn in praise of Chairman Mao.

Chairman Mao is Praised on Five Continents

A Chinese satellite soars through the heavens,
Everywhere in the universe "The East is Red" can be heard.
People on five continents and four seas are celebrating,
People worldwide are raising their voices together in song:
Long Live, Long Live the Communist Party!
Long Live, Long Live Chairman Mao!

By the Sixth Grade (1) Class of Number Three Primary School, Luxiangyuan Road, South District, Shanghai.

The Peoples of China and Albania are the Closest of All

Red satellite, glowing in the dark
Please deliver a message for me:
When you fly over Albania
Tell the courageous red "Mountain Eagles"
That our hearts are joined as one.
As anti-imperialists and anti-revisionists we carry out revolution together,
Shoulder to shoulder, we unite in the struggle:
The peoples of China and Albania are the closest of all.

Cultural Revolution 1966–76

Ah Bei: A Young South Vietnamese Soldier. Shandong People's Publishing Company, 1973.

The enemy had advanced to the bank of the stream, where they discovered a young boy with a water bottle. They asked him: "Did you see anyone pass by here?" The little boy pointed in the direction of the south.

Uncle nimbly strolled up beside him and said: "Ah! Play your mouth organ, Ah Bei, let the song of our national liberation resound through all the mountains and rivers of our motherland."

The Story of Norman Bethune, A Proletarian Internationalist Soldier. Zhejiang People's Press, 1971.
A comic book rendition of the heroic exploits of Dr. Norman Bethune, a Canadian who aided the communists in Yanan. Chairman Mao later immortalized Bethune in one of his most famous short essays.

Cultural Revolution 1966–76

1. ***English, Volume I, Shanghai Primary Schools.* Shanghai Primary and Middle School Textbook Compilation Group. Shanghai, September 1969.**
   Lesson One of the English textbook used in Shanghai primary schools during one of the most virulently ideological years of the Cultural Revolution. The Chinese inscription under Mao's picture reads: "Chairman Mao Zedong is the greatest Marxist-Leninist of the present age – Lin Biao." Two years after this was published, Lin Biao died after carrying out an unsuccessful coup on Chairman Mao's life, according to official sources.

2. ***English, Volume I, Shanghai Middle Schools.* Shanghai Primary and Middle School Textbook Compilation Group, Shanghai, August 1969.**
   Lesson One of the English textbook used in Shanghai Middle Schools in 1969. The middle-school text goes slightly further than the primary school version. The text in the box is identical to that in the primary school textbook. The banners hanging from balloons read, from left to right: "Long Live the Chinese Communist Party," "Wishing Chairman Mao a Long Life," "Long Live Chairman Mao," and "Long Live Chairman Mao's Thought."

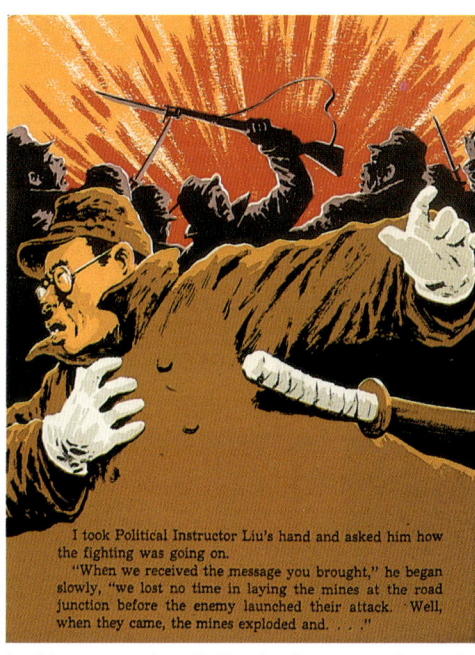

3. ***Observation Post 3.* Foreign Language Press, Beijing, 1960; this edition reprinted 1972.**
   A war story set in World War II in China.

4. ***Beijing Youth* magazine. Beijing, May 1974.**
   The cover picture shows students holding signs that read: "We are the little generals who are criticizing Lin Biao and Confucius;" "Criticize Lin Biao, Criticize Confucius, oppose revisionism, defend yourself from revisionism;" Open fierce fire against Lin Biao and Confucius..."

Cultural Revolution 1966–76

Will the Real Lei Feng Please Stand Up?

Lei Feng, a common solider and truck driver in the People's Liberation Army, is the best known hero in the Chinese communist propaganda pantheon. Lei Feng is famous for his selflessness, succinctly expressed in his vow, "I wish only to be a small screw in the revolution," and by his early death by electrocution when he backed his truck into a power line during a storm. Lei Feng is principally a children's hero in China. His life and good deeds have been extolled in countless stories, songs, comic books, films, textbooks and classroom posters since the 1960s. Many books and posters extolling Lei Feng continue to be published in the late 1990s. Mao Zedong launched a "Study Comrade Lei Feng" movement, and Mao's calligraphy of this slogan often adorns photographs and paintings of the hero.

A selection of stories, comics, film music songbook and a bookmark from 1963 to 1990.

Cultural Revolution 1966–76

Cultural Revolution 1966–76

Little Red Guard magazine. Shanghai, February 25, 1972.

Our Extracurricular Activities

Top from left: Study, Showing conciliation to families of victims or model heroes, Labor
Bottom from left: Propaganda work, Sports, Sentry duty

Little Red Guard magazine. Shanghai, April 10, 1971.

Never Forget Class Struggle

The capitalist roaders are still on the road,
The capitulationists are still capitulating,
Never give up class struggle, never give it up,
Raise high the great banner of Marxism and Leninism,
Fight on, fight on, fight on!

Cultural Revolution 1966-76

Little Red Guard magazine. Shanghai, June 10, 1970.

Peoples of the world, unite! Defeat the American invaders and all their running dogs!

Youth and Children Pictorial magazine. Tianjin, July 1960.
Cover picture captioned "Smash American Imperialism's Plot to Start a New War" U.S. President Dwight Eisenhower, depicted as an intimidated rat, flees at the sight of a ethnically diverse proletarian mob from China, Vietnam, the Middle East and Russia.

Cultural Revolution 1966–76

Little Red Guard Pictorial magazine. Tianjin, June 1971.

Included in the text (not shown) is the clarion call: "Children of the world, unite! Thoroughly wipe out imperialists, revisionists, and counter-revolutionaries." The boy wearing the white Muslim cap is holding a sign that reads: "Down with American imperialism! Down with Soviet revisionism!"

Little Red Guard magazine. Shanghai, July 25, 1971.

Learn from the People's Liberation Army.

Little Red Guard magazine. Shanghai, March 25, 1972.

Cultural Revolution 1966–76

A selection of children's songbooks from before and during the Cultural Revolution.

Songs for Little Companions

Open Fire to Criticize Lin Biao and Confucius

Little Red Guand Dance Dramas

Little Red Guard Dance Dramas

Post-Cultural Revolution 1977–99

Little Red Guard magazine. Shanghai, September 9, 1977.

The period 1977–78 can be called the Hua Guofeng interregnum, between the long decades of Mao Zedong's rule and the opening up of China to the outside world under Deng Xiaoping. Ideologically, Hua has more in common with Mao than with Deng, and during his brief reign, he fitted quite neatly into Mao's propagandistic shoes. One characteristic of the Deng era, which began in 1978 after the fall of Hua, was the absence of visual propaganda, and a conspicuous effort to avoid fostering leadership worship.

The hearts of the children of Taiwan are with the Communist Party.
The sign on the fence reads "Taiwan Provincial Government." The sign the children unfurl reads: "Warmly celebrate the triumphant opening of the Eleventh National Party Congress." The sign they surreptitiously attach to the guard's back reads "Liberate Taiwan."

The young coach sums up: "Today's drill went very well! Little Hua was quite brave. Our training is not simply to build up health! We want to learn to 'fear neither hardship nor death' as well."

Start Early to Build Good Health. Foreign Language Press, Beijing, 1978.

Calendar book for May 4, 1982. No place, no publisher.
To commemorate the anti-imperialist May Fourth movement in 1919 in which many students and women as shown in the drawing participated, the day is celebrated as Youth Day in China. The date in the lunar calendar is also given, the 11th day of the fourth month.

Archer Yi Shoots Down the Nine Suns. People's Art Publishing Company, Beijing, 1984.
Illustrated version of an ancient myth in which the Shang-dynasty archer Yi kills nine out of the ten suns in the sky, thus terrifying the remaining sun into shining.

The ten sun brothers wreak havoc in the heavens. They grow increasingly wild and fierce. Their mother pursues them in a chariot, but they play hide and seek with her. There is nothing she can do to control them.

Their unbridled behavior causes great suffering to the common people. Their light and heat combine into one vast force, which is terrifying and devastating in its intensity. Before long, the earth's crust splits into pieces. The rivers dry up, the plants die and all the leaves wither on the trees. A severe drought threatens all mankind.

Ideology and Ethics textbook, Full Time Primary Schools, Volume 3. People's Education Press, Hubei, 1988.
Using this picture, the student is asked to explain family relationships. By 1988, ten years after the one-child-family policy was instituted, nearly all urban families had only one child.

Above the picture: *Do you know the relationships among these people, and the proper form of address for each of them? Discuss the relationships among the members of your own family.*

Below the picture: *When you run into the following situations, how do you respond?*

1. When you come home after school, you are very, very hungry, but Grandmother hasn't cooked dinner yet. What do you do?

2. Your father offers to carry your book bag for you and accompany you to school. How do you respond?

3. You are having a wonderful time playing outside, when your mother calls you and asks you to go shopping for food with her. How do you respond?

Post-Cultural Revolution 1977–99

Nature and Common Knowledge. *Shanghai, Xinhua Bookstore, 1994.*
The 1980s saw the appearance of familiar commercial products in textbooks.

做个"线电话",用线电话做传声游戏。

42

Make a "string telephone" and play with it to demonstrate the transmission of sound.

Arithmetic. *Shanghai Scientific and Technical Education Press, Shanghai, 1989.*

说一说什么比什么高,什么比什么矮。

哪几个站错了位置,他们应该排在哪里?

2

Top: Which is taller, which is shorter?
Bottom: Determine which child is standing out of order, and then put them in the proper order.

General Knowledge for Pre-school Children. Volume 2. *People's Education Press, Changsha, Hunan, November, 1989.*

我爱解放军

解放军叔叔我爱你,
我把鲜花献给你。

I love the People's Liberation Army.

Uncle PLA soldier, I love you. This gift of flowers is for you.

88

Post-Cultural Revolution 1977–99

***Thinking and Behavior. Primary 2, First Semester.* Shanghai Xinhua Bookstore, 1994.**
Negative examples.

Left:
1. On a cold day, grandma tells Lili to put on her sweater. Lili says: "What a bother."
2. Dongdong says: "Grandma, help me find my writing brush. I have to practice my calligraphy."

Right: *Thinking and Doing.* Look at the picture and explain why, in the old society, fathers and mothers gave their children away, sold them or discarded them.

***Learning to Read by Looking at Pictures.* Volume 2. Tibet People's Publishing Company, Lhasa. 1990.**
An illustrated glossary in Tibetan, Chinese and *pinyin*.

Top left to right: *Planting trees for reforestation. Plowing the earth. Flying a kite.*
Bottom left to right: *Bouncing a ball. Washing clothing. Playing billiards.*

89

Post-Cultural Revolution 1977–99

***Art for Pre-school Classes, Volume 2.* Xinjiang Youth Press, 1989/1993.**
Translated into Uighur from the Chinese-language edition.

***Young Deng Xiaoping.* Central Archives Publishing Company, Beijing, 1998.**
His grandmother and his mother worried that he was too young to go on such a long trip, but he insisted that he wanted to go and finally got his way.

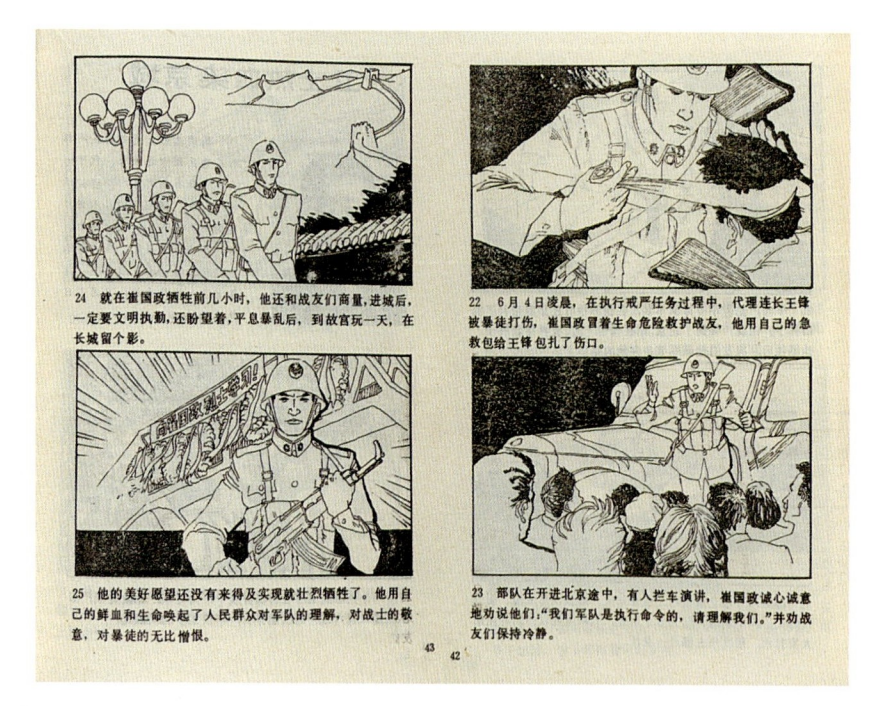

***Heroic Defenders of the Republic.* China Youth Daily Publishing Company, Beijing, September 1998.** A comic book that presents the government's line on the Tiananmen Square massacre, June 4, 1989.

22. Early in the morning of June 4, while enforcing martial law, acting company commander Wang Feng was injured by the thugs. Cui Guozheng risked his life to save his comrade in arms. He used his own personal first aid kit to treat Wang Feng's injury.

23. As the army moved into Beijing, people blocked the trucks carrying troops, and started to give lectures to all bystanders. Cui Guozheng sincerely tried to persuade the crowds to get out of the way: "The army is only trying to follow orders. Please try to understand us." He also urged his comrades to remain calm.

24. Only hours before Cui Guozheng sacrificed his life, he was holding discussions with his fellow soldiers. He told them that once they entered the city of Beijing, they must carry out their duties in a civilized manner. He also hoped that after suppressing the insurrection, he would be able to spend a day sightseeing in the Forbidden City, and having his photograph taken at the Great Wall of China.

25. But before he could realize these hopes, Cui Guozheng sacrificed his life to a noble cause. By giving up his own blood and life, he aroused the masses' understanding of the army, their respect for the soldiers and their undying hatred of the thugs.